Deutsch direkt! WORKBOOK

Margaret Wightman

BBC Books

1 Guten Tag

1 In German there is more than one word for both *the* and *a*. Nouns may be masculine, feminine or neuter, singular or plural.
See page 16 of the *Deutsch direkt!* course book:

(m) **der**   (f) **die**   (n) **das**   (pl) **die**
    ein   **eine**   **ein**

Fill in the gaps:

i   **der**, **die** or **das**?

    a   Wo ist _____ Böttcherstraße?

    b   _____ Stadtplan ist alt.

    c   _____ Kirche ist auf der rechten Seite.

    d   Wo ist _____ Verkehrsverein?

    e   _____ Strandhotel ist gleich hier links.

ii   **ein** or **eine**?

    a   Bremen ist _____ Stadt in Norddeutschland.   die Stadt

    b   Wo ist hier _____ Friseur?   der Friseur

    c   Catherin ist _____ Mädchen.   das Mädchen

    d   Drüben ist _____ Bank.   die Bank

    e   Auf dieser Seite ist _____ Hotel.   das Hotel

2 If you want a specific place like the station or the town hall ask:
Wo ist der/die/das . . .?
Wo sind die . . . ? if it is plural.
If you simply want any post office, hotel, hairdresser etc ask:
Wo ist (hier) *eine* Post?
Wo ist (hier) *ein* Hotel? etc

    Ask for:

a das Hotel Stern	*d* die Drogerie	*g* die Rathausstraße
b der Dom	*e* das Stadttheater	*h* der Bahnhofsplatz
c die Bank	*f* die Toiletten	*i* die Bremer Stadtmusikanten

3 After **ich** almost all verbs end in **-e**
after **wir** and **Sie/sie** they end in **-en**
e.g. ich *wohne*   wir *wohnen*
            Sie/sie *wohnen*

Complete these descriptions people gave of themselves.
Use these verbs to complete each description, in this order:
heißen   kommen   wohnen   machen

a Peter Fürst   Ich _____ Peter Fürst.
       aus Heidelberg   _____ aus Heidelberg.
       in Bremen   _____ in Bremen.
       Urlaub in England   _____ Urlaub in England.

b Marianne Meyer   Ich _____
       aus Erfurt   _____
       in Berlin   _____
       Urlaub in Duhnen   _____

c Elfriede und Wilhelm Richter   Wir _____ Richter, Elfriede
                                                              und Wilhelm Richter.
       aus Cuxhaven   _____
       in Hamburg   _____
       Urlaub in Heidelberg   _____

d The next person doesn't introduce
       himself at all.
       Find out his name   Wie _____ ?
       where he's from   Woher _____ ?
       and where he lives   Wo _____ ?

4 One common verb does not follow the above pattern; it is **sein** *to be*, which is a law
unto itself.
The forms of it which you meet in Chapter 1 are:

ich *bin*   **wir** *sind*
er/sie/es *ist*   **Sie/sie** *sind*

Fill in the gaps with the appropriate part of **sein**:

a Wie alt _____ Sie, Frau Debus?

b _____ Sie hier auf Urlaub?

c Frau Michaelis, das _____ Sebastian.

d Entschuldigen Sie bitte, wo _____ die Kirche?

e Wir _____ hier, und Duhnen _____ hier.

f Ich _____ aus Bremen.

g Wo _____ die Bremer Stadtmusikanten?

5i Many questions begin with a special 'question word' or phrase such as **Wo . . . ?**
Wie . . . ?   Woher . . . ?.   They are followed by the verb.

Fill in the gaps with one of the above question words:

a _____ ist Erfurt?

b _____ heißen Sie?

c _____ wohnen Sie hier in Duhnen?

d _____ ist Ihr Name?

e _____ kommen Sie?

f _____ alt sind Sie?

ii Questions which can be answered by *yes* or *no* begin with a verb; the subject follows the verb:

e.g. *Sind* **Sie aus dieser Stadt?**

Turn these statements into questions:

EXAMPLE **Sie macht in Duhnen Urlaub.**
  Macht sie in Duhnen Urlaub?

a Sie wohnt im Strandhotel. _____

b Erfurt ist in der DDR. _____

c Sie heißen Joachim. _____

d Das ist Sebastian. _____

e Sie sind hier auf Urlaub. _____

6i **Er**, **sie** and **es** are masculine, feminine and neuter respectively. They are used to replace **der**, **die** and **das** words. **Er** and **sie** also replace a man's or woman's name.

e.g. **Wo ist** *das Hotel Parzival?* *Es* **ist gleich um die Ecke.**

Plural words (or several names) are all replaced by **sie**, regardless of gender.

Fill in the gaps with **er**, **sie** or **es**:

a Wie alt ist das Parlament? _____ ist sehr modern.

b Wo sind denn die Bremer Stadtmusikanten? _____ sind hinter dem Rathaus.

c Der Roland ist sehr alt, _____ ist fünfhundert Jahre alt!

d Wie alt ist Herr Kothe? _____ ist vierunddreißig.

e Wo ist Susanne? _____ ist auf dem Marktplatz.

ii After **er/sie/es** verbs end in **-t**; after **Sie/sie** they end in **-en**.

e.g. **er/sie/es** *wohnt* **Sie/sie** *wohnen*

Look again at Exercise 3 on page 8 and complete the descriptions using **er/sie/es** or **sie** as appropriate:

a _____ Peter Fürst. *b* _____ *c* _____

 _____ aus Heidelberg. _____ _____

 _____ in Bremen. _____ _____

 _____ Urlaub in England. _____ _____

7 Write the numbers in figures in the boxes:

a Sebastian ist sieben Jahre alt.

b Herr Kummer macht acht Tage Kurzurlaub.

c Die Böttcherstraße ist siebzig Jahre alt.

d Die Insel Neuwerk ist dreizehn Kilometer von Duhnen entfernt.

e Heide Debus ist dreiundvierzig Jahre alt.

f Joachim Kothe ist vierunddreißig Jahre alt.

g Ernst Brütt hat zwei Wagen und sechs Pferde.

h Frau Brütt hat zwölf Ferienwohnungen.

i Frau Else Schricker ist über achtzig Jahre alt.

2 *Volltanken, bitte*

---

1 Two of the most common verbs do not follow the usual pattern:

haben *to have*	**sein** *to be*
ich *habe*	ich *bin*
du *hast*	du *bist*
er/sie/es/man *hat*	er/sie/es/man *ist*
wir/Sie/sie *haben*	wir/Sie/sie *sind*

Fill the gaps with the appropriate part of **haben** or **sein**:

a _____ Sie Briefmarken?

b Wie alt _____ du?

c Ich _____ dreiundvierzig Jahre alt.

d Sie _____ einen Garten.

e Sebastian, _____ du noch Geschwister?

f _____ Sie aus Bremen?

g Bremen _____ eine alte Stadt.

h Ich _____ kein Auto, aber Heide _____ einen Ford.

i Entschuldigen Sie, bitte, wo _____ das Rathaus?

---

2 After **es gibt** . . . , **(wo) gibt es** . . . ? or any part of **haben**,
ein (m) becomes **einen**
ein (n) and **eine** (f) don't change.
Remember: **ein** has no plural form; just leave it out.

i You're enquiring about these places of interest in the town you're visiting.

EXAMPLE **Gibt es hier in Memmingen** *einen* **Markt?** *market*

a Gibt es _____? *cathedral*

b _____? *theatre*

c _____? *restaurant beneath the town hall*

d _____? *park*

e _____? *museum*

f _____? *art gallery*

ii   Fill in the gaps with **einen**, **eine** or **ein**:

    a Sebastian, hast du _____ Schwester?

    b Heide hat _____ Mantel.

    c Haben Sie _____ Stadtplan von Bremen?

    d Ich habe _____ Sohn und _____ Tochter.

    e Marion Michaelis hat _____ Auto.

    f Hat Frau Hadrian _____ Videorekorder?

    g Sie hat _____ Fahrrad, _____ Fernseher, _____ Radio und _____ Stereoanlage.

    h Haben Sie _____ Briefmarken? [Careful!]

3 **Kein**, *not any, none*, is a neat way of saying you haven't got something. It adds the same endings as **ein** in the singular; in the plural it's **keine**.

Fill in the gaps with **keinen**, **keine**, or **kein**:

    a Sebastian hat einen Bruder, aber er hat _____ Schwester.

    b Wir haben _____ Stadtpläne und auch _____ Briefmarken.

    c Frau Hadrian hat _____ Videorekorder, _____ Auto, _____ Waschmaschine und _____ Geschirrspülmaschine.

4 German nouns often form their plurals by adding **-e**, **-n**, **-en** or **-er**. Some also change the vowel in the middle of the word: **u** to **ü**, **o** to **ö**, or **a** to **ä**; if the change is in a word containing **-au-** it's the **a** that changes: **-äu-**. Some words do not change at all; a very few add **-s**.

In a compound noun such as **Hausfrau**, only the last element changes: **Hausfrauen**.

Show the plurals of these words:

die Kirche _____	der Kiosk _____	der Mann _____
das Hotel _____	das Theater _____	der Garten _____
der Stadtplan _____	die Postkarte _____	das Apartmenthaus _____
der Markt _____	der Supermarkt _____	das Café _____
die Stadt _____	die Briefmarke _____	das Rathaus _____

5i In a statement the order of words may change, but the verb is always the second element, though not always the second word.

e.g. **Eine Stereoanlage** *habe* **ich auch.**

    Ich *habe* **auch eine Stereoanlage.**

Unscramble these sentences in two different ways:

    a Heide Debus
        jetzt   _____ in Lilienthal bei Bremen.
        wohnt   _____ in Lilienthal bei Bremen.

    b gibt
        in Bremen _____ viele Cafés.
        es   _____ viele Cafés.

    c das Rathaus
        Sie   _____ dort drüben.
        sehen   _____ dort drüben.

ii In a question where there is no question word, the verb always comes first.
To turn a statement into a question, begin with the verb:
e.g. **In Lilienthal *gibt* es eine Schule.**
   ***Gibt* es in Lilienthal eine Schule?**

Rewrite the examples in part i of this exercise as questions:

a _____?

b _____?

c _____?

6 Study the verbs printed at the bottom of page 31 of the *Deutsch direkt!* course book.
They are: **kommen   machen   wohnen   schreiben   heißen   arbeiten**

Man is the equivalent of English *one, you, they* or *people*.

Fill in the gaps with the correct part of one of the above verbs; some are needed
more than once:

a Das _____ man JOACHIM.

b Herr Kothe _____ an einer Schule. Er ist Lehrer.

c Volltanken, bitte, Super. Was _____ das, bitte?

d Woher _____ Sie, Herr Kummer?

e Wir sind hier auf Urlaub. Wir _____ im Strandhotel.

f Wie _____ dein Bruder?

g Ich _____ Hadrian, Trudel Hadrian.

h _____ Sie ganztags im Puppentheater, Frau Spilker?

i Sebastians Papa _____ Wolfgang.

j _____ du aus Bremen, Jan Ole?

k Marion Michaelis _____ in einer Wohnung in der Wernigeroder Straße.

7 **Liegen, spielen, kaufen, trinken, gehen, finden** follow the same pattern as the verbs in
Exercise 6 (above).

Fill in the gaps with the correct part of one of these verbs; some are needed more
than once:

a Bremen _____ in Norddeutschland.

b Joachim _____ Benzin.

c Frau Spilker _____ Puppentheater.

d Wir _____ Blumen, Obst und Gemüse.

e Ich _____ in den Verkaufsraum.

f Sie _____ die Apotheke auf der rechten Seite.

g Sebastian und Jan Ole _____ mit den Skulpturen im Skulpturgarten.

h Wir sitzen in der Sonne und _____ Bier.

3 Wo kann ich . . . ?

1 To ask the price of a single item:
Was kostet *der*? (m)
Was kostet *die*? (f)
Was kostet *das*? (n; also used for entry fees etc.)

To ask the price of several identical items:
Was kosten *die*?

If you want to know the total cost of several items:
Was macht *das*?

Complete the sentences below using one of the above expressions:

a Diese Blumen sind schön!   Was _____ ?

b Eine Postkarte?   Ja, bitte. Was _____ ?

c Sie möchten also diesen Stadtplan.   Ja. Was _____ ?

d Man kann das Rathaus besichtigen.   Gut. _____ ?

e Möchten Sie diese kleine Scholle?   _____ ?

f Man kann ein Fußballspiel besuchen.   Prima. _____ ?

g Für Sie eine Tasse Kaffee, für Sie
ein Bier und für Sie ein Eis mit Sahne.   Danke schön. _____ ?

h Entschuldigen Sie! Die Erdbeeren – was _____ ?

2 In the 'third person singular' verbs end in **-(e)t**
e.g. **er/sie/es/man** *heißt, kostet, spielt*

The 'third person plural' ends in **-en**
e.g. **sie** *heißen, kosten, spielen*.

Wolfgang and Susanne Mönch are on holiday in Bremen.

Here Wolfgang is talking about himself:

Ich heiße Wolfgang Mönch und ich bin 42 Jahre alt. Ich wohne in Beuel bei Bonn, aber ich arbeite in Köln. Ich habe ein Auto, einen Ford. Im Moment sitze ich in einem Café und schreibe eine Postkarte nach England.

Susanne joins in:

Wir sind auf Urlaub hier in Bremen. Heute machen wir eine Hafenrundfahrt, dann trinken wir im Hotel Columbus eine Tasse Kaffee. Heute abend essen wir im Ratskeller, dann gehen wir ins Theater.

Rewrite Wolfgang's passage in the 'third person singular', beginning **Er . . .** and Susanne's in the 'third person plural', beginning **Sie . . . .**

3 **Fahren**, **geben** and **essen** do not follow the normal pattern for verbs. There is a changed vowel when they are used with **du**, **er/sie/es/man**, or with a noun. See page 48 of the *Deutsch direkt!* course book.

Vowel changes in the present tense are shown in the glossary to *Deutsch direkt!* in brackets like this: **fahren (ä)**, **geben (i)**.
If there is a further change, the 'third person' is shown in full: **essen (ißt)**.

Fill in the correct part of **fahren**, **geben** or **essen**:

a ＿＿＿＿＿＿ Sie mir bitte sechs zu einer Mark.

b Du ＿＿＿＿＿ hier rechts und dann wieder rechts.

c Ich ＿＿＿＿＿ ein Erdbeereis mit Sahne.

d ＿＿＿＿＿＿ es in Bremen einen Dom?

e Heide ＿＿＿＿＿ nach München.

f Wir ＿＿＿＿＿ direkt in die Stadt.

g ＿＿＿＿＿＿ du gern Kohl und Pinkel?

h Im Winter ＿＿＿＿＿ die Familie Brütt in Urlaub.

i Uwe Debus ＿＿＿＿＿ eine Kutterscholle.

j Die Wattwagen ＿＿＿＿＿ von Duhnen zur Insel Neuwerk.

4 After **kann** the verb which completes the meaning comes right at the end,
e.g. **In Bremen kann man eine Hafenrundfahrt** *machen.*
Man kann in dem sehr schönen Bürgerpark *spazierengehen.*

Cologne's an interesting town.

Match the verbs on the left with the correct activity, then write a sentence about each of the activities you can do there. The first one has been done for you.

besichtigen	ins Theater	**gehen**
gut einkaufen	einen Ausflug in das Siebengebirge	＿＿＿＿
ansehen	den Dom und das Rathaus	＿＿＿＿
machen	am Rhein	＿＿＿＿
gehen	in den Kaufhäusern	＿＿＿＿
spazierengehen	eine Dampferfahrt auf dem Rhein	＿＿＿＿
machen	ein Fußballspiel im Müngersdorfer Stadion	＿＿＿＿

In Köln kann man ins Theater gehen. Man kann ＿＿＿＿＿＿＿＿＿＿＿＿＿＿＿＿

＿＿

＿＿

＿＿＿＿＿＿＿＿＿＿＿＿＿＿＿＿＿＿＿＿＿＿＿＿＿＿＿＿＿＿＿＿＿＿ usw

5 After **kann** the verb which completes the meaning comes right at the end.

You're now visiting Munich. You need to know:

a what you can do   **Was kann man hier machen?**

b where you can park   ＿＿＿＿＿＿＿＿＿＿＿＿＿＿＿?

c where you can get a good meal   ＿＿＿＿＿＿＿＿＿＿＿＿＿＿＿?

d where you can go for a walk   ＿＿＿＿＿＿＿＿＿＿＿＿＿＿＿?

e where's a good place to go shopping   ＿＿＿＿＿＿＿＿＿＿＿＿＿＿＿?

f what you can see at the theatre (**im Theater**)   ＿＿＿＿＿＿＿＿＿＿＿＿＿＿＿?

g if you can look round the town hall   ＿＿＿＿＿＿＿＿＿＿＿＿＿＿＿?

h if you can take a steamer trip   ＿＿＿＿＿＿＿＿＿＿＿＿＿＿＿?

6 To tell someone to do something, begin with the verb:
e.g. *Kommen Sie* **bitte hierher!**

Turn the verbs listed on the right into instructions, and fit them into the correct sentence:

EXAMPLE *Gehen Sie* **links rum und dort ist das Postamt.**   Sie kommen

a	_____ mir bitte sechs Briefmarken zu einer Mark.	Sie machen
b	_____ bitte herein, Herr Kothe!	Sie bringen
c	_____ uns mal wieder, Frau Debus!	Sie gehen
d	_____ , haben Sie einen Stadtplan?	Sie fahren
e	_____ mir bitte einen Weißwein.	Sie sagen
f	_____ mit der Straßenbahn in die Stadt.	Sie besuchen
g	_____ einen Ausflug nach Bremen!	Sie geben

7 One way to ask a question is to use a 'question word' which is immediately followed by the verb.
e.g. *Wo* **wohnen Sie hier in Duhnen?** *Wie alt* **sind Sie, Herr Kothe?**

i Using these 'question words', complete the examples below:
wo wie wie alt was für ein . . . woher was

a _____ heißt du?

b _____ kommen Sie?

c _____ schreibt man das?

d _____ bist du, Sebastian? Bist du schon sieben?

e _____ ist Ihr Name?

f _____ ist Erfurt?

g _____ macht das, bitte?

h _____ gibt es hier in der Nähe einen Supermarkt?

i _____ Auto haben Sie?

j _____ ist die Nummer, HB-KD 281 oder 182?

k _____ ist Ihr Traumauto? Ein Ford?

l _____ Stadt ist Bremen?

ii You're talking to Trudel Hadrian and the conversation turns to the subject of Joachim Kothe. Ask Frau Hadrian:

a how old he is   _____

b where he lives   _____

c where he works   _____

d where he's from   _____

e if he has a car   _____

f what sort of car he has   _____

4 Haben Sie ein Zimmer frei?

NEW WORD
die Großeltern (pl) *grandparents*

---

1 **Nehmen** and **sehen** have changed spellings after **du**, **er/sie/es/man**:

ich nehme	**ich** sehe
du *nimmst*	**du** *siehst*
er/sie/es/man *nimmt*	**er/sie/es/man** *sieht*
wir/Sie/sie nehmen	**wir/Sie/sie** sehen

i   Fill in the gaps with the appropriate form of **nehmen**:

a Ich _____ Zucker und Sahne. _____ Sie auch Sahne?

b Ich esse ein Stück Himbeertorte. Was _____ du?

c Und Rolf, was _____ er?

d _____ Sie ein Glas Tee oder ein Kännchen?

e Möchten Sie die Zimmer haben? Ja, die Zimmer _____ wir.

ii   Fill in the gaps with the appropriate form of **sehen**:

a _____ du den Hund? Er heißt Wastl.

b Im Schnoor _____ man Silvia Kirsch bei der Arbeit.

c _____ Sie die Kirche? Die Post ist direkt gegenüber.

d Ach ja, die Stadtpläne _____ ich dort drüben!

e Was _____ wir heute abend im Theater?

---

2 **Ich möchte** etc is part of the verb **mögen** and says what someone *would like*. It is the only verb of its type you need to use at this stage:

ich *möchte*
du *möchtest*
er/sie/es/man *möchte*
wir/Sie/sie *möchten*

Sometimes another verb at the end of the sentence completes the meaning:
e.g. **Heide möchte nach München** *fahren.*

Fill the gaps with the appropriate form of **mögen**:

a Frau Hadrian _____ sechs Briefmarken zu siebzig.

b _____ Sie Sahne dazu?

c Ich _____ gerne die Rechnung.

d Welchen Kuchen _____ du?

e Was _____ Catherin trinken?

f Wir _____ bitte frühstücken.

3 After verbs such as **haben**, **nehmen** and **mögen** masculine determiners change:
der to **den**, ein to **einen**, kein to **keinen**, ihr to **ihren** etc.
e.g. **Rolf hat** *einen* **Hund** (einen Hund is the 'direct object' of this sentence; it is said to be in the *accusative case*).
Feminine and neuter determiners and all plurals do not change.

Add the correct endings:

a Catherin Debus möchte ein____ Ceylontee und ein____ Stück Himbeertorte. Heide nimmt d____ Herrentorte. Catherin ist Heides Tochter. Heide hat auch ein____ Sohn, Karsten und ein____ Hund.

b Marion Michaelis ist nicht verheiratet, sie hat kein____ Kinder und auch kein____ Hund. Sie hat aber ein____ uraltes Auto.

c Sie möchten ein____ Doppelzimmer mit Dusche, und ein Einzelzimmer? Ein____ Doppelzimmer habe ich in der fünften Etage. D____ Einzelzimmer ist in der vierten Etage. Möchten Sie d____ Zimmer haben? Schön.

4 **Mein** takes the same endings as **ein** or **kein**. For details see page 293 of the *Deutsch direkt!* course book.

You're showing off the family photo album.
Add the correct form of **mein**, and the appropriate pronoun:

EXAMPLE **Das ist** *meine* **Mutter.** *Sie* **ist leider tot.**

a Das ist _____ Vater. _____ wohnt seit vier Jahren in Cambridge.

b Das sind _____ Großeltern. _____ sind achtzig Jahre alt.

c Hier sehen Sie _____ Frau. _____ heißt Peggy.

d Das sind _____ Kinder. _____ gehen schon zur Schule.

e Sehen Sie _____ Hund? _____ kommt aus Bayern!

f Das ist _____ Haus. _____ ist wirklich sehr alt.

g Hier sehen Sie _____ Auto. _____ ist ja uralt! _____ Traumauto ist ein Mercedes Sportwagen!

5 **Sein** *his*, **ihr** *her, their*, **Ihr** *your* take the same endings as **mein**. For details see page 293 of the *Deutsch direkt!* course book.

Fill the gaps with **sein**, **ihr** or **Ihr** adding the correct endings:

EXAMPLE **Das ist Wolfram. Das ist** *sein* **Haus, und das hier ist** *seine* **Mutter.**

a Helmut hat eine Katze. _____ Katze heißt Muschi.

b Inge hat auch eine Katze. _____ Katze heißt Minka.

c Inge hat auch drei Kinder. _____ Söhne heißen Klaus und Richard, _____ Tochter heißt Silvia.

d Frau Debus, Sie haben zwei Kinder, ja? Wie heißen _____ Kinder?

e Die Ungers haben auch zwei Kinder. Wie alt sind _____ Kinder?

f Detlef hat ein neues Auto. _____ Auto ist ein Ford.

g Petras Auto ist kein Ford. _____ Auto ist ein Mercedes.

h Ernst Brütt hat sechs Pferde. _____ Pferde heißen Max, Theo, Hans, Cäsar, Susi und Püppi.

6 When you're talking about quantities, there is never any word for 'of':
e.g. **eine Tasse Tee, hundert Gramm Schinken**
In the plural masculine and neuter quantities do not change:
e.g. **zwei** *Stück . . .* , **drei** *Kännchen . . .* , **vier** *Glas . . .*
Feminine quantities have their normal plural:
e.g. **zwei** *Flaschen . . .* , **drei** *Tassen . . .*

You're a large group in the **Konditorei** and everyone wants something different.
Fill in what you all want:

Wolfgang möchte _____ (*a bottle of beer*).

Susanne _____ (*a glass of orange juice*).

Uwe und Elke _____
    (*two pots of coffee and one slice of raspberry flan*).

Heide _____
    (*a slice of Black Forest gateau and a cup of coffee*).

Sebastian _____
    (*two slices of marzipan cake with cream and a glass of milk*).

Catherin _____ (*a glass of tea with lemon*).

Karsten _____ (*a slice of cheesecake*).

---

7 Ask the lone young man sitting opposite you in the café:

a where he comes from   _____

b if he lives in Bonn   _____

c whereabouts in Bonn he lives _____

d does he have a house or a flat _____

e what sort of car he has   _____

f if he is married   _____

g how long he's been married   _____

h what his wife is called   _____

i what her job is   _____

j if he has any children   _____

k do they go to school   _____

l how old they are   _____

m what they are called   _____

n what there is to do in Bonn _____

---

8 German nouns form their plurals in various ways (see Chapter 2, Exercise 4).
Those which end in **-in** double the 'n' and add **-en: die Verkäuferinnen**.
Some ending in **-um** change the last two letters: **das Museum, die Museen**.

Show the plurals of these words:

die Marke _____   die Nacht _____   die Kellnerin _____

die Mark _____   die Tasse _____   das Haustier _____

der Fahrplan _____   der Brief _____   das Zimmer _____

der Schlüssel _____   der Pfirsich _____   das Kind _____

die Tochter _____   das Gymnasium _____   die Sekretärin _____

das Radio _____   das Fahrrad _____   der Gasthof _____

5   Ich hätte gerne . . .

1 Adjective endings vary according to whether they are used with **der**, **die**, **das** or with **ein**, **eine** etc
e.g. **der** *alte* **Mann**   **ein** *alter* **Mann**
　　das *alte* **Haus**   **ein** *altes* **Haus**
For a full table see page 296 of the *Deutsch direkt!* course book.

When **sauer** and other adjectives ending in **-er** add an ending, they often drop an 'e'
e.g. **sauer**, **der** *saure* **Regen**, **die** *sauren* **Äpfel**

Answer the questions:

EXAMPLE **Möchtest du ein kleines Eis?**　**Nein, ein** *großes*.　(groß)
　　　Nehmen Sie die gelben Pfirsiche?　**Nein, die** *weißen*.　(weiß)

a Möchten Sie eine große Flasche Bier?　Nein, _____　(klein)

b Möchten Sie die süßen Kirschen?　Nein, _____　(sauer)

c Hätten Sie gern einen grauen Pullover?　Nein, _____　(weiß)

d Trinken Sie gern einen trockenen Wein?　Nein, lieber _____　(süß)

e Möchtest du das kleine Stück?　Nein, _____　(groß)

f Nehmen Sie den weißen Kandis?　Nein, _____　(braun)

2 If an adjective is not immediately in front of the noun it is used in its basic form without any ending at all.
e.g. **Das Wetter ist** *wechselhaft*. **Die Firma Bünting ist** *alt*.

Adjectives formed from place names end in **-er**. They never change.
e.g. **Marion wohnt in der** *Wernigeroder* **Straße.**

Fill in the gap with the adjective given in brackets, supplying the ending where necessary:

a Ich esse lieber einen _____ Apfel.　(sauer)

b Trinken Sie Ihren Kaffee gern _____ ?　(schwarz)

c Diese Banane esse ich nicht. Sie ist noch _____ !　(grün)

d Was kosten die _____ Rosen? Und die _____ ?　(gelb, rot)

e Sind diese Äpfel _____ oder _____ ?　(süß, sauer)

f Der Frankenwein hier ist ein _____ Rosenberg, ja?　(Sommerach)

g Diese Himbeertorte schmeckt _____ !　(lecker)

h Der Bremer trinkt gern einen _____ Ostfriesentee.　(kräftig)

i Die _____ Bäckerei in Greetsiel ist sehr _____ .　(alt, klein)

j Ich hätte gern einen _____ _____ Wein.　(trocken, badisch)

3 If the thing you want has already been mentioned, or if you can point to it, there is no need to repeat the name.

Say **(ich nehme)** *den* (m)
die (f and pl)
das (n)

Complete the following sentences, using the appropriate part of **nehmen** plus **den**, **die** or **das**:

EXAMPLE **Diesen Frankenwein kann ich empfehlen.**   *Den nehmen wir.*

a Diese Scholle ist ganz frisch.   Gut, ich _____ .

b Der Stadtplan kostet zwei Mark, ja?   _____ ich, bitte.

c Dieses Brot ist noch warm.   _____ ich.

d Das Zimmer kostet DM 40 mit Frühstück.   _____ wir.

e Möchten Sie diese Rosen?   Nein, wir _____ hier.

f Das ist ein guter Wein?   Dann _____ ich _____ .

4 Adding **gern**, **lieber** or **am liebsten** to a verb transforms the meaning:

ich trinke Bier   *I am drinking beer*
ich trinke *gern* Bier   *I like (drinking) beer*
ich trinke *lieber* Bier   *I prefer beer, I'd rather have beer*
ich trinke *lieber* Bier *als* Kaffee   *I prefer beer to coffee*
ich trinke *am liebsten* Bier   *I like beer most of all*

NB **Gern** does not replace the verb.

Using these verbs: **arbeiten, essen, spielen, trinken, wohnen**

a Say you prefer:

   meat to fish   _____

   working in Germany to England   _____

   living in Bremen to Greetsiel   _____

   playing tennis (**Tennis**) to football   _____

b Ask your companion if he/she:

   likes orange juice   _____

   likes cheese   _____

   prefers working in a school   _____

   would rather have a scrambled egg   _____

c Say you like these things best of all: _____

   Black Forest gateau   _____

   coffee with sugar and cream   _____

   staying in a hotel   _____

   playing chess   _____

5 To express a definite time when an event took (or takes) place, or a definite length of time, use the accusative case:

e.g. **Kommen Sie *jeden Tag* hierher? Das ist nicht weit, nur *zwei Minuten* zu Fuß.**

NB There is no word for *for*.

Complete these sentences; the time you need is given in English:

a Die Fahrt von Duhnen zur Insel Neuwerk dauert _____ .   *for four hours*

b Bei Bünting bin ich jetzt _____ .   *for 17 years*

c _____ trinke ich zwei Tassen Kaffee.   *every morning*

d Die Dorfkirche in Dötlingen ist _____ alt.   *900 years*

e Der Chor singt _____ einmal.   *every week*

f Wir machen hier _____ Kurzurlaub.   *for eight days*

g _____ von hier entfernt wohne ich.   *ten minutes*

6 **Das** and **es** can be followed by a plural verb if the item they refer to is plural.

Compare: **Was ist ein Shanty? *Das ist* ein Arbeitslied.**

            Was sind Shantys? *Das sind* Arbeitslieder.

Fill the gaps with **es kann, es können, das ist, das sind**:

EXAMPLE **Wieviele Tassen Tee trinken Sie? *Es können* zehn Tassen sein.**

a Die Herrentorte, was ist das? _____ Schokoladensahne mit Weinbrand abgeschmeckt.

b Max, Theo, Hans, Cäsar, Susi und Püppi: _____ die Pferde von Herrn Brütt.

c Sieben Mark und eine Mark zehn, _____ zusammen acht Mark und zehn.

d Was wir fangen? _____ Seezungen und Schollen und Aale.

e Das Wetter ist sehr wechselhaft. _____ tagelang regnen.

f Ich serviere viele Kännchen pro Tag, _____ dreißig oder vierzig werden.

7 Select the correct number(s) from each group to complete these statements and write them in both words and figures:

a Mit _____ Jahren ist man noch ein Teenager.   neunzehn / neunzig / neun

b _____ Gramm ist mehr als _____ .   siebenundfünfzig / fünfundsiebzig

c Der Wein kostet vier Mark siebzig. Ah, Sie haben ein Fünfmarkstück. Sie bekommen _____ Pfennig zurück.   dreizehn / dreißig / drei

d Mein Vater ist sehr alt, er ist _____ Jahre alt.   achtzehn / achtundsechzig / sechsundachtzig

e Catherins Tulpen kosten _____ das Stück.   neunzig Mark / neunzig Pfennig

f Zwei Mark fünfzig und fünf Mark sechzig sind zusammen _____ .   sieben Mark neunzig / acht Mark zehn / sieben Mark fünfundsiebzig

g Das Doppelzimmer kostet pro Person dreißig Mark. Dazu kommt noch das Frühstück, also zweimal acht Mark. Das macht zusammen _____ .   achtunddreißig Mark / sechsundvierzig Mark / sechsundsiebzig Mark

8 In *seven* of the groups below there is an item which does not fit with the quantity given;
in the eighth group all the items match the stated quantity.
List the 'odd ones out', and decide which group is entirely correct:

a	ein Kilo	Birnen Weinbrand Zucker	*e*	ein Glas	Marmelade Weißwein Bier mit Schuß
b	ein Stück	Kandis Marzipankuchen Sahne	*f*	ein Liter	Milch Zitronen Wein
c	ein Kännchen	Rotwein Ostfriesentee Kaffee	*g*	zehn	Schokolade Eier Brötchen
d	ein Paket	Äpfel Ostfriesenmischung Kandis	*h*	100 g	Pfirsiche gekochten Schinken Tee

6   *Wie komme ich . . . ?*

NEW WORD
die Fähre (-n)   *(cross-channel) ferry*

---

1 The dative case is always used after these prepositions:
aus bei gegenüber mit nach seit von zu

In the dative case masculine and neuter determiners end in **-em**
feminine determiners end in **-er**
plural determiners end in **-en**
most plural nouns add **-(e)n**:

e.g. **Nach *dem* Frühstück machen wir eine Hafenrundfahrt.**

Add the correct endings:

a Wohin fahren Sie mit Ihr____ Auto?

b Im Schnoor sieht man die Künstler bei d____ Arbeit.

c Wenn Sie aus d____ Bahnhof rauskommen, gehen Sie immer geradeaus.

d Wohnen Sie weit von d____ Innenstadt?

e Ich verbringe meine Freizeit mit mein____ Familie.

f Seit ein____ Jahr wohnen wir in Dötlingen.

g Geben Sie mir bitte sechs Briefmarken zu ein____ Mark.

h Die Steenblocks gehen mit ihr____ vier Kinder____ in die Kirche.

---

2 If you're going places it's:
nach for towns, villages, suburbs, and *most* countries
zu for all other places such as buildings, streets and squares

zum (= **zu dem**) with masculine and neuter nouns
zur (= **zu der**) with feminine nouns
zu den with plural nouns

Ask how you get to these places:

EXAMPLE **Wie komme ich *zur* Sögestraße?**   *Sögestraße*

a _____   *Leer*

b _____   *Wernigeroder Straße*

c _____   *the market square*

d _____   *the Weser bridge*

e _____   *Bremer Stadtmusikanten*

f _____   *Lilienthal*

g _____   *the island of Neuwerk*

3 The dative case is used after these prepositions when they describe where things are:
an   auf   hinter   in   neben   über   unter   vor
e.g. **In *meiner* Gemeinde wohnen etwa viereinhalbtausend Menschen**.

(See Chapter 10, Exercise 2, for more about these prepositions with the accusative.)

Add the missing prepositions and the correct endings:

a _____ ein____ Jahr fahre ich 20 000 Kilometer.   *in*

b Die Brauereigaststätte ist direkt _____ d____ Brauerei.   *next door to*

c Der Schnoor liegt _____ d____ Postgebäude.   *behind*

d Das große Geschäft _____ d____ Ecke ist Karstadt.   *at*

e Die Waage? Die steht _____ d____ Rathaus.   *in front of*

f Man kann _____ d____ Bürgerpark spazierengehen.   *in*

g Ich stehe hier _____ d____ Marktplatz von Bremen.   *in* [careful!]

4 Possessives refer to the person speaking (*I/my, you/your* etc):

mein	(ich)	*unser* (wir)
dein	(du)	*Ihr* (Sie)
sein	(er, es)	*ihr* (sie)
ihr	(sie)	

Possessives are determiners and take the same endings as **ein/kein**; for details see page 293 of the *Deutsch direkt!* course book.

Fill in the gaps with the correct possessive; add the appropriate ending:

EXAMPLE **Heide hat zwei Kinder. *Ihr* Sohn heißt Karsten, und *ihre* Tochter heißt Catherin.**

a Was machen Sie in _____ Urlaub?

b Na, Sebastian, wie heißt denn _____ Papa? Und _____ Mami?

c Herr und Frau Steenblock gehen mit _____ vier Kindern in die Kirche.

d Wir sind seit 1895 Schwarzbuntzüchter in _____ Familie.

e _____ Name ist Herbert Kummer. Ich komme aus Minden in Westfalen.

f Ich bekomme _____ Glasstäbe aus Deutschland.

g Jan Gosselaar ist Fischer, wie _____ Vater vor ihm.

h Wie viele Leute arbeiten auf _____ Boot, Herr Gosselaar?

5 Words expressing a more general time when something repeatedly happens, add **-s**; they are written with a small letter:
e.g. **mittags, abends, nachts, montags, werktags**

Complete these sentences; the time you should include is given in English:

EXAMPLE **Der Chor singt *abends* (*in the evenings*) von zwanzig Uhr bis zweiundzwanzig Uhr.**

a Das Geschäft ist _____ (*in the afternoons*) von vierzehn bis achtzehn Uhr geöffnet.

b Die Vorstellungen sind zweimal in der Woche, _____ (*on Wednesdays*) und _____ (*on Fridays*).

c Inge Ysker trinkt Kaffee _____ (*in the mornings*) als Muntermacher.

d _____ (*on Sundays*) geht die Familie Steenblock in die Kirche.

e Arbeiten Sie auch _____ (*nights*)?

f _____ (*at midday*) esse ich immer in einem Restaurant.

g Herr Herlyn melkt seine Kühe _____ (*in the mornings*) und _____ (*in the afternoons*).

6 German has three words for *where*: **wo**, **wohin** and **woher**:
wo is used when no movement is involved
wohin strictly means *where to*
woher means *where from*

Supply the correct word:

a _____ kommen Sie, Frau Hadrian?

b _____ fahren Sie im Urlaub?

c _____ wohnen Sie hier in Leer?

d _____ gibt es hier eine Apotheke?

e _____ kommt Ihr Mann?

f _____ kann ich eine Tasse Kaffee trinken?

g _____ verreisen Sie am liebsten, Frau Michaelis?

h _____ haben Sie Stadtpläne?

7 **Wissen** and **halten** have a changed spelling after **du** and **er/sie/es/man**. See page 92 of the *Deutsch direkt!* course book.

Fill in the gaps with the correct part of **wissen**:

a Wir _____ nicht, wohin wir im Sommer verreisen.

b _____ du, wie oft man die Kühe melkt?

c Ich _____ , wie man nach Spetzerfehn kommt.

d _____ Sie, was das Nationalgetränk in Ostfriesland ist?

e Jan Ole _____ nicht, was Piccadilly ist.

Fill in the gaps with the correct part of **halten**:

f Jan Ole, was _____ du von England?

g Was _____ Gerhard Herlyn von seinem Beruf?

h _____ _____ ich von meinem Mercedes Sportwagen? Das ist ja mein Traumauto!

i _____ _____ Sie von Spanien, Frau Michaelis?

j _____ _____ wir von *Deutsch direkt!*? Es ist einfach ausgezeichnet.

8 If you're going places on foot, it's **gehen**.
If you're using transport it's **fahren**.
To say you're on foot it's **zu Fuß**.
To say what transport you're using it's **mit . . .** (with the dative case):
e.g. **Möchten Sie** *zu Fuß gehen* oder *mit dem* **Auto** *fahren?*

Remember: In German word order the way you're travelling (*how*) always comes before your destination (*where*).

Using the English cues below, say where you're going:

EXAMPLE **I'm going to Munich by train.**   *Ich fahre mit dem Zug nach München.*

a to the park by bike   Ich _____

b by bus to Greetsiel   _____

c to the shopping centre on the tram   _____

d on foot to the car park   _____

e to Berlin by train   _____

f on the ferry to Dover   _____

g on the number 4 to the station   _____

h by car to the landing stage   _____

i by steamer to Bremerhaven   _____

7 Zweimal Bonn, bitte

NEW WORDS
einfahren *to drive in, enter, arrive*
einsteigen *to board a vehicle*

---

1 Many verbs separate into two parts in the present tense:
e.g. **aufstehen** **Ich** *stehe* **um sieben Uhr** *auf.*
umsteigen *Steigen* **Sie in München** *um*!

Supply the correct version of the verb given in brackets:

a Der nächste Zug (abfahren) um dreizehn Uhr.

b Wann (ankommen) der Zug in Frankfurt?

c Die Marktfrauen (aufstehen) um vier Uhr.

d Um wieviel Uhr (anfangen) wir mit der Arbeit?

e (Aussteigen) Sie am Marktplatz?

f Marions Mittagspause (ausreichen) nie.

g Ich gehe in die Stadt. (mitkommen) Sie?

h Du (herauskommen) aus dem Bahnhof, dann gehst du nach links.

i Guten Tag. (hereinkommen) Sie bitte!

---

2 You need to recognise the 'infinitive' of a separable verb in order to look it up in a dictionary or the Glossary of **Deutsch direkt!** The 'infinitive' is the basic form of a verb; it almost always ends in -en, e.g. **ausreichen**, **umsteigen**.

Identify the separable verbs in this passage and list their 'infinitive' forms:

Ich stehe um sechs Uhr auf und fahre mit dem Bus in die Stadt. Mein Mann kommt auch mit. Wir steigen am Bahnhof aus. Auf Gleis 3 fährt der Zug aus Düsseldorf ein. Mein Mann und ich steigen schnell ein.

Ich fahre heute nach Beuel. Leider kann ich nicht direkt fahren – der Zug hält ja nicht in Beuel – ich muß also in Köln umsteigen. Mein Mann steigt aber in Köln aus. Er fängt schon um halb acht mit der Arbeit an.

Der Zug nach Beuel fährt von Gleis fünf. Er fährt pünktlich ab und kommt zwanzig Minuten später in Beuel an. Um Viertel vor acht komme ich aus dem Bahnhof heraus. Meine Kollegin steht vor dem Bahnhof und wir gehen zusammen zur Arbeit.

---

3 In the present tense separable verbs split.
After **können** and **müssen** the two parts join up.
Compare: **Wann** *steht* **sie** *auf*? **Wann muß sie** *aufstehen*?

What was the question?

EXAMPLE *Wann fährt der Zug ab?* **Der Zug fährt in fünf Minuten ab.**

a _____ ? Der Bus kommt um 20 Uhr in Bonn an.

b _____ ? Wir steigen hinter dem Rathaus aus.

c _____ ? Ich stehe um Viertel vor sechs auf.

d _____ ? Wir fangen spät an, um neun Uhr.

EXAMPLE *Wo muß ich umsteigen?* **Sie müssen in München umsteigen.**

e _____ ? Herr Mönch kann am Freitag vorbeikommen.

f _____ ? Ich muß um halb fünf aufstehen.

g _____ ? Sie können schon heute anfangen.

4 If something takes place *at* a time by the clock, the time is preceded by **um**:
e.g. *um* **vier Uhr**

From one time *to* another is **von . . . bis**:
e.g. *von* **drei Uhr nachmittags** *bis* **ein Uhr nachts**

Fill in the gaps with the most appropriate word (**um, von, bis**):

a Gerhard Herlyn melkt die Kühe nachmittags _____ 17 Uhr und morgens _____ 5.30 Uhr.

b Der nächste Zug nach Salzburg fährt _____ acht Uhr neun.

c Marion Michaelis steht _____ halb acht auf.

d Am Wochenende schläft sie gern _____ elf, halb zwölf.

e Das Frühstück esse ich _____ Viertel vor acht.

f Der Bremer Ratskeller ist _____ 10 _____ 24 Uhr geöffnet.

g Die Marktfrau bleibt _____ sechs Uhr abends.

h Der Residenzgarten öffnet _____ 9.30 Uhr.

5 Fill the gap with the most appropriate question word from this list:

wann	wie	wieviel	wo
was	wie alt	wie viele	woher
was für	wie lange		wohin

a _____ trinken Sie lieber, Milch oder Orangensaft?

b _____ können wir frühstücken? Geht es schon um sieben?

c _____ bist du denn Sebastian? Sieben schon? Ein ganz großer Junge, ja!

d _____ Brötchen möchten Sie, zwei oder drei?

e _____ wohnt Jan Oles Brieffreund, in Epping oder in London?

f _____ serviert man ostfriesischen Tee, mit Kandis und Sahne oder ohne?

g _____ haben Sie Feierabend?

h _____ einen Hund haben Sie, Frau Debus?

i _____ kommen diese Erdbeeren?

j _____ arbeitet Herr Langwisch schon bei Bünting?

k _____ Urlaub haben Sie im Jahr?

l _____ fährst du, Jan Ole? Nach England?

m _____ öffnet die Post an Wochentagen?

n _____ Taschengeld hat Jan Ole?

6 **An** means *on* a particular day and *at* the weekend; it is followed by the dative:
e.g. *An welchem Tag fahren Sie nach Cuxhaven?*
In the singular **an dem** is usually shortened to **am**:
e.g. *am* **Samstag**, *am* **Wochenende**

i   Answer the questions about the coming week's activities like this:
Wann gehen Sie zum Friseur?   *Am Dienstag gehe ich zum Friseur.*

MO	4	*18.00 Tennis*
DI	5	*10.30 Friseur*
MI	6	*Fahrkarten kaufen*
DO	7	*6.30 nach Würzburg*
FR	8	*Würzburg bis 19.00*
SA	9	*Einkaufen u. Gartenarbeit*
SO	10	*Gartenarbeit u. Tennis*

a An welchen Tagen sind Sie in Würzburg?
_____

b Wann kaufen Sie die Fahrkarten?
_____

c Wann spielen Sie Tennis?
_____

d Wann machen Sie Gartenarbeit?
_____

e An welchem Tag stehen Sie früh auf?
_____

ii   In the dative plural most nouns end in -**(e)n**:
e.g. **An welche*n* Tag*en* sind Sie in Würzburg?**

Give the German for these phrases:

EXAMPLE **on Sundays** *an Sonntagen*

a on weekdays _____
b at the weekends _____
c on Tuesdays _____

d on public holidays _____
e on closing days _____
f on Fridays _____

7 Separable verbs split in the present tense, but not in the infinitive:
e.g. *einsteigen*   ich *steige . . . ein*   ich kann hier *einsteigen*

Answer the questions fully, incorporating the information given in English.

EXAMPLE **Wo steigen wir ein?**   *(in Duhnen)*
         Wir steigen in Duhnen ein.

a Fangen Sie morgens um acht Uhr an?
   Nein, ich _____   *(no, at 8.30)*

b Um wieviel Uhr kommt die Fähre aus Harwich an?
   Die Fähre aus Harwich _____   *(at two in the afternoon)*

c Wann fährt der Bus nach Oberneuland ab?
   Der Bus nach Oberneuland _____   *(at 10.05)*

d Wann kann der neue Kellner anfangen?
   Der neue Kellner _____   *(on Wednesday)*

e Muß ich in Ulm umsteigen?
   Nein, Sie _____   *(no, in Neu-Ulm)*

8 When adjectives are used after a noun they need no ending.

When used before a noun the ending depends on the type of determiner, and the number, gender and case of the noun.
For further details see page 296 of the *Deutsch direkt!* course book.

From the list in the box select the most appropriate adjective to fill each gap, and add the correct ending:

a Die Marktfrauen arbeiten nicht am Sonntag. Die Woche ist _____ genug.

b Möchten Sie eine _____ Fahrt oder eine Rückfahrkarte?

c In Südspanien hat man eine _____ Landschaft.

d An einem _____ Tag arbeitet Herr Steenblock oft bis zehn Uhr abends.

e Das Gemüse auf dem Markt ist immer sehr _____ .

f Zum Frühstück esse ich ein _____ Ei.

windreich
lang
frisch
einfach
weichgekocht
wunderschön

8 *Grüß Gott!*

NEW WORDS
die Fremdsprache (-n) *foreign language*
die Muttersprache (-n) *native language*
Russisch *Russian language*
das Wort (-e) *word*

---

1 When there is no determiner, the adjective endings vary according to the number, gender and case of the noun.
For details see page 297 of the *Deutsch direkt!* course book.

Fill the gaps with the correct endings:

a In Regensburg gibt es hübsch_____ Geschäfte.

b Im Schnoor kann man modern_____ Schmuck und frisch_____ Brot kaufen.

c Karstadt und Horten und Hertie sind drei groß_____ Kaufhäuser.

d Schwarz_____ Kaffee schmeckt Frau Michaelis am besten.

e Wir haben heute frisch_____ Erdbeeren mit Vanilleeis und Sahne.

f Wechselhaft_____ Wetter ist typisch für Bremen.

g Windreich_____ Tage gefallen Theo Steenblock.

h Die Männer in dem Shanty-Chor haben verschieden_____ Berufe.

2i To say you're from a certain country: **aus**
with feminine countries: **aus der**
with plural countries: **aus den**
For further details see page 114 of the *Deutsch direkt!* course book.

At an international congress your colleagues are introducing themselves, saying also where they're from:

EXAMPLE **Ich bin Maddalena. Ich komme *aus Italien.***

a Mein Name ist Moritz. Ich komme _____ Schweiz.

b Ich heiße Juan Ramon Sanchez. _____.

c Ich bin Igor. _____.

d Mein Name ist Pierre. _____.

e Ich heiße Aileen McKechnie. _____.

f Ich bin Chuck Kissinger und das ist mein Kollege Walt Whitman Junior.

Wir _____.

g Mein Name ist Stavros. _____.

h And finally, introduce yourself _____.

ii To talk about going to most countries: **nach**
       with feminine and plural countries: **in die**

     Fill the gap with the correct word(s):

     a   Marion Michaelis fährt gern _____ Südspanien.

     b   Jan Ole möchte gern _____ England fahren.

     c   Im Winter fahren wir oft _____ Schweiz.

     d   Möchten Sie _____ Sowjetunion fahren?

     e   Im Frühjahr machen viele Norddeutsche einen Ausflug _____ Holland.

---

3   Adjectives of 'nationality' (**deutsch**, **englisch**, **ostfriesisch** etc) never have a capital letter:
e.g. **Wastl ist ein** *bayrischer* **Name**.

Adjectives of nationality are normally written with a capital letter when used as the name of a language:
e.g. **Ich lerne** *Deutsch*.
But they have a small letter when they describe *how* you say something:
e.g. **Wie heißt Köln** *auf englisch*? **Wie sagt man** *rice auf chinesisch*?
These languages are mentioned in *Deutsch direkt!*: **Chinesisch, Deutsch, Englisch, Französisch, Griechisch, Italienisch, Latein, Spanisch**: new is **Russisch**.

     Complete these sentences with the appropriate language or adjective from those listed above:

     a   Marie-Claire wohnt in Frankreich. Dort spricht man _____ .

     b   Heide Debus kommt aus der DDR. Ihre Muttersprache ist _____ .

     c   Richard Kerler studiert zwei alte Sprachen. Er studiert _____ und _____ .

     d   Citroën und Renault sind _____ Autos.

     e   Munich heißt _____ München.

     f   Ich fahre sehr gern nach Italien. Das _____ essen schmeckt mir ausgezeichnet.

     g   In der Sowjetunion spricht man _____ .

     h   Frau Michaelis findet Südspanien wunderschön. Leider spricht sie kein Wort _____ .

     i   Der Sommeracher Rosenberg ist ein _____ Wein.

---

4   After **ich möchte** etc the verb expressing *what* you'd like to do is in the infinitive form; it comes at the end of that part of the sentence (i.e. of that clause).
e.g. **Was möchtest du** *essen*?

     You and your friends are discussing holiday plans. Say what everyone wants to do, using the information below and the most appropriate verb from those listed in the box.

     EXAMPLE   **Marianne** *möchte* **in York Jorvik** *besichtigen*.

Pierre: Bremen – Kohl und Pinkel	besichtigen
Bernd: Moskau – der Kreml	besuchen
Barbara: die USA – Disneyland	essen
Wolfgang und Elke: Österreich – Winterurlaub	fahren
Paul: Greetsiel – ostfriesischer Tee	machen
Mein Mann und ich: Hamburg – Hotel Vier Jahreszeiten	trinken
Jan Ole: England – sein Brieffreund in Epping	übernachten
Marion: Südspanien – ins Innere	verdienen
Richard: Regensburg – Geld	

5 **Ich möchte** etc is followed by an infinitive at the end of the clause.
The same word order applies after
müssen (the infinitive describes *what you have to do*)
können (it denotes *what you can do*)
wollen (it says *what you want to do*)

Answer the questions in full sentences incorporating the information given in English.

EXAMPLE **Wann kann Frau Müller vorbeikommen?**   (*next week*)
Frau Müller kann nächste Woche vorbeikommen.

a Was will Richard werden? _____   (*a teacher*)

b Wo möchte Angelika arbeiten? _____   (*in industry*)

c Wohin möchte Heide fahren? _____   (*to Basle*)

d Wo muß Martin umsteigen? _____   (*in Milan*)

e Wo kann man hier gut einkaufen? _____   (*in the Sögestraße*)

f Wann muß Herr Haberland aufstehen? _____   (*at 5.30*)

g Wann können wir frühstücken? _____   (*from 6 to 9*)

h Wie lange kann sie bleiben? _____   (*an hour*)

6 To say in a particular month or season it's **im**:
e.g. **im August**, **im Sommer**

The list of birthdays in your diary looks like this:

Angelika	12.04
Bärbel	17.01
Christoph	5.02
Dorle	6.10
Harald	12.12
Michael	21.02
Trudi	30.12
Papa	1.05
Herr Greiner	31.03
ich	25.03

Wann haben sie Geburtstag?

EXAMPLE **Angelika hat *im April* Geburtstag.**

a Bärbel _____

b Christoph und Michael _____

c Dorle _____

d Harald und Trudi _____

e Papa _____

f Herr Greiner und ich _____

7 To give your opinion or find out what someone thinks use **glauben**:
e.g. *Ich glaube, daß* ich in Bremen etwas *finde.*
Glauben Sie, daß es überall gleich schwer *ist?*
After **daß** the verb comes at the end of that part of the sentence.

EXAMPLE *I think Jan Ole will go to Epping.*
Ich glaube, *daß* Jan Ole nach Epping *fährt.*

Say you think that:

a Trudi will become a teacher   Ich glaube, daß _____

b you'll stay until Tuesday   _____

c you (and your partner) will go to Scotland _____

d Angelika will find a job in Würzburg   _____

e *Deutsch direkt!* is excellent   _____

8

Es ist	schwierig,	eine Arbeit zu finden.
		eine Arbeitsstelle zu bekommen.
	leicht,	Lehrer zu werden.

In sentences of this type **zu finden**, **zu bekommen** and **zu werden** come at the end.
Finden, **bekommen** and **werden** are in the infinitive form.

You're listening to a student telling you about some of his problems; complete his story using these verbs: **arbeiten, finden, studieren, suchen, verdienen, wohnen**

Es ist frustrierend, _____ (*looking for a room*

in the town centre). Es ist teuer, _____ (*living in Munich*),

aber es ist leicht, _____ (*to earn money*).

Es ist unmöglich, _____ (*to work every day*).

Es ist besser, _____ (*to work at*

weekends or in the university vacations). Es ist interessant, _____

(*studying German and history*) aber es ist nicht leicht, _____

(*to find a job in industry*).

9 Darf ich?

---

1 **Dürfen** *to be allowed to*: see page 130 of the *Deutsch direkt!* course book.

After **dürfen** the verb expressing *what you are allowed to do* comes at the end and is in the 'infinitive' form.

Answer these questions in full, adding the information in brackets:

EXAMPLE **Wieviel Kuchen dürfen Sie bei dieser Diät essen?** (gar keinen)
Bei dieser Diät *dürfen* **wir gar keinen Kuchen** *essen*

a Wieviele Kalorien darf Christina pro Tag essen?

Pro Tag _____. (tausend)

b Darf man Gift trinken?

Nein, Gift _____.

c Darfst du Alkohol trinken?

Ja, ich _____. (ein Glas Weißwein)

d Dürfen wir hier parken?

Nein, hier _____.

e Wie oft darf mein Mann Kuchen essen?

Er _____. (1x Woche)

f Wie lange dürfen Ihre Kinder aufbleiben?

Sie _____. (bis 21 Uhr)

g Was dürfen Sie zum Frühstück essen?

Zum Frühstück _____. (ein Ei)

---

2 **Müssen** *to have to*: see page 132 of the *Deutsch direkt!* course book.

After **müssen** the verb expressing *what you have to do* comes at the end and is in the 'infinitive' form.

Answer these questions in full, adding the information in brackets:

EXAMPLE **Wann muß Ihr Sohn ins Bett gehen?** (um Viertel vor zehn)
An Wochentagen *muß* **er um Viertel vor zehn ins Bett** *gehen*.

a Wann mußt du nach Wien fahren?

Im Mai _____.

b Wie oft müssen Sie Gymnastik machen?

Ich _____. (2x am Tag)

c Muß ich eine Diät machen?

Ja, leider _____.

d Wieviel Wasser muß Ihre Frau trinken?

Sie _____. (300 Kubikzentimeter)

    e Wie lange muß er in Italien arbeiten?

      Er _____ . (bis Ende Mai)

    f Müssen wir mit dem Arzt einen Termin ausmachen?

      Ja, mit _____ .

    g Was mußt du heute kaufen?

      Heute _____ . (Brot, Obst, Milch)

    h Um wieviel Uhr muß ich aufstehen?

      Sie _____ . (4.30)

3 **Können** *to be able to*: see page 129 of the *Deutsch direkt!* course book.

After **können** the verb expressing *what you are able to do* comes at the end and is in the 'infinitive' form.

Answer these questions in full, adding the information in brackets:

EXAMPLE **Kann man das Wasser gut trinken?** (sehr gut)
Hier *kann* man das Wasser sehr gut *trinken*.

    a Wo kann man hier gut essen?

      Hier _____ . (im Ratskeller)

    b Du kannst gut singen, oder?

      Oh ja, ich _____ . (sehr gut)

    c Was kann man in Bad Mergentheim machen?

      In _____ . (eine Trinkkur)

    d Können Sie in der Mittagspause vorbeikommen?

      Nein, in _____ .

    e Kann Richard in Regensburg eine Arbeitsstelle finden?

      Nein, in Regensburg _____ .

    f Wann kann ich kommen?

      Sie _____ . (morgen vormittag um 10 Uhr)

    g Können Sie Fahrrad fahren, Frau Hadrian?

      Selbstverständlich _____ .

    h Sag mal, Wolfgang, wann können wir dieses Jahr Urlaub machen?

      Dieses Jahr _____ . (im März oder im Mai)

4 After **dürfen**, **können**, **müssen** the verb which completes the meaning comes at the end and is in the 'infinitive' form.

Supply the correct part of the most appropriate verb from **dürfen**, **können**, **müssen**:

    a Sebastian _____ um Viertel nach acht ins Bett gehen.

    b Mein Mann nimmt Schlaftabletten. Im Moment _____ er nicht Auto fahren.

    c Ich mache Diät. Ich _____ überhaupt kein Fett essen.

    d Ihre Kinder gehen aber noch nicht zur Schule. _____ sie schon Skilaufen?

    e _____ dein Sohn gut schwimmen?

f Manchmal gehen die Puppen kaputt; Frau Spilker _____ sie dann reparieren.

g Bitte schön? Was _____ es sein?

h Es tut mir leid, nächsten Dienstag _____ ich arbeiten.

i Entschuldigen Sie bitte, hier _____ Sie nicht rauchen.

j Die Patienten, die Gewichtsprobleme haben, _____ Diät essen.

k Brötchen haben wir leider nicht. _____ es auch ein Weißbrot sein?

---

5 To say *of the* use the 'genitive' case. The genitive determiners are:
des, eines etc with masculine and neuter nouns; the nouns add **-s** or **-es**
der, keiner etc with feminine and plural nouns, which do not change
e.g. **Die Patienten machen im Laufe *des Vormittags* noch Gymnastik.**
   Morgens Fango, abends Tango: das ist der Lieblingsspruch *unserer Gäste*.

Fill the gaps using the genitive case of the words listed on the right:

a Die Kirche im Zentrum d____ _____ ist neunhundert Jahre alt.   das Dorf

b Der Pfarrer dies____ _____ ist Wilfried Waschek.   die Kirche

c Wie lange arbeiten Sie schon im Garten d____ _____?   die Residenz

d Einige mein____ _____ wohnen hier im Sanatorium.   der Patient

e Das ist nicht in der Nähe d____ _____.   die Innenstadt

f Die Patienten warten auf die Visite d____ _____.   der Arzt

---

6 To tell someone *to do something* you need part of the verb known as the 'imperative'.
There are three forms:
e.g. **machen Sie . . . !** used to people you address formally
   mach . . . ! to a child, a member of the family, a pet or a friend
   macht . . . ! to several children, pets, friends etc

machen Sie! is the '**Sie form**' of the verb in reverse
mach! is based on the '**du form**' of the verb i.e. **du machst, du nimmst, du ißt, du schläfst**; there is sometimes an extra **-e**. Any vowel change in the '**du** form' is normally kept, though a change involving only an **Umlaut** is dropped:
e.g. *Nimm dir einen Apfel und iß schnell!* BUT *Schlaf gut!*
macht! is the '**ihr form**' of the verb without the pronoun

Supply the appropriate imperative form of the verb in brackets:

a (geben) _____ mir bitte Ihre Fahrkarte!

b (kommen) _____ Sebastian, (sagen) _____ Mama eben gute Nacht.

c Tschüs, Wolfgang. (fahren) _____ nicht zu schnell!

d (trinken) _____ das Wasser, Hildegard, es ist gesund!

e (kommen) _____ ihr Kinder, es gibt Eis!

f Nach Spetzerfehn wollen Sie? (fahren) _____ hier immer geradeaus!

7 To talk about a single occasion:

heute	vormittag
morgen	nachmittag
Montag	abend

the same thing each week:

vormittags	montags
nachmittags	Montag abends
abends	

Fill the gaps with the 'time' phrase suggested by the words in brackets:

a Die Patientin möchte _____ (*this afternoon*) einen Termin bei
   Herrn Doktor Bergis haben.

b Sebastian hat _____ (*tomorrow*) zur ersten Stunde Unterricht.

c Kann ich _____ (*Monday morning*) um neun Uhr kommen?

d _____ (*this evening*) gehen einige Patienten ins Kino.

e Dr Bergis hat _____ (*in the mornings*) von 8 Uhr bis 10 Uhr und
   _____ (*in the afternoons*) von 3 bis 6 Uhr Sprechstunde.

f Michael kann _____ (*tomorrow morning*) einen Termin haben.

g Die Patienten müssen _____ (*in the mornings*) Gymnastik machen.

h _____ (*on Wednesday afternoons*) hat Dr Salzer keine
   Sprechstunde.

i Tee trinkt Marion Michaelis am liebsten _____ (*in the evenings*).

j _____ (*on Sundays*) arbeitet Herr Steenblock nicht.

10 *Zum Wohl!*

NEW WORDS
der Tafelwein   *table wine*
wer? *who?*

---

1 With these prepositions the accusative case is always used:
bis durch entlang für gegen ohne um
For accusative determiners see page 293 of the *Deutsch direkt!* course book.

Fill in the correct endings:

a Gehen Sie d____ Sögestraße entlang!

b Wir organisieren sportliche Aktivitäten für unser____ Gäste.

c Für ein____ Führung bekommt Richard vierzig Mark.

d In Bremen kann man einen Spaziergang durch d____ Bürgerpark machen.

e Die Bremer Stadtmusikanten sind um d____ Ecke.

f Für d____ Trinkkur bekommt jeder Gast sein eigenes Glas.

g Kann man hier durch d____ Innenstadt fahren?

h Für mein____ Vater kaufe ich einen Frankenwein.

i In Dötlingen gehen die Touristen durch d____ Dorf spazieren.

---

2 Some prepositions can be followed by both the accusative and the dative.
Those used in *Deutsch direkt!* are:
an auf hinter in neben über unter vor zwischen

When they answer the question **wo . . . ?** a dative follows:
e.g. *Im* Schnoor gibt es viel zu kaufen.
 Hoch über *der* Stadt steht die Festung Marienberg.
If they answer the question **wohin . . . ?** they need an accusative:
e.g. Zuerst kommt Kandis in *die* Tasse.
 Man gießt den Tee über *den* Kandis.

Fill in the gaps with the correct case of **der, die, das, ein** etc:

a Hier darf man nicht über _____ Straße gehen.

b Wir wohnen in ein____ Ferienwohnung.

c Hinter _____ bunten Gebäude finden Sie einen Parkplatz.

d Die Keller befinden sich unter _____ Residenz zu Würzburg.

e Gehen Sie bitte in _____ Verkaufsraum. Dort haben wir Stadtpläne.

f In Jever ist die Brauereigaststätte gleich neben _____ Brauerei.

g Man hört die Musik der Drehorgeln auf _____ Straßen Bremens.

h Im Zentrum von Bremen liegt vor _____ Rathaus der alte Marktplatz.

i Sie kommen wieder rechts auf _____ Osterdeich.

j Bei schönem Wetter sitzen die Touristen an _____ Strand.

k Heute steht der Dom zu Würzburg wieder wie vor _____ Krieg.

l Möchten Sie in _____ ersten Klasse fahren?

3 In their comparative form most adjectives end in **-er**.
They add a further ending in exactly the same way as ordinary adjectives:
e.g. **Herr Unger möchte gern ein** *neueres* **Auto haben.**

These single-syllable adjectives also add an **Umlaut**:
alt groß hart jung kalt kurz lang nah schwarz stark warm
e.g. **Sebastian hat einen** *älteren* **Bruder.**

Adjectives ending in **-el**, **-en** and **-er** drop the '**e**':
e.g. **teuer,** *teurer*

A few comparisons are irregular; those you meet in *Deutsch direkt!* are:
gut, *besser*; **hoch,** *höher*; **viel,** *mehr* (never changes!)

> Complete these sentences using the comparative form of the adjective:
>
> *a* Ostfriesland ist (flach) _____ als Franken.
>
> *b* Der Kabinett ist süß, die Spätlese ist aber _____ .
>
> *c* Sebastian ist (jung) _____ als Jan Ole.
>
> *d* Der (flach) _____ Wein ist der Müller-Thurgau.
>
> *e* Der Müller-Thurgau ist (billig) _____ als der Kabinett.
>
> *f* Das Rathaus zu Bremen ist alt, der Dom ist aber noch viel _____ .
>
> *g* Die gelben Tulpen sind (schön) _____ als die weißen.
>
> *h* Welches Hotel ist (teuer) _____, der Schützenhof oder das Hotel Columbus?
>
> *i* Die (gut) _____ Studenten bekommen auch keine Arbeitsstelle.

4 Most adjectives form their superlative by adding **-st** before the normal adjective ending:
e.g. **die schönsten Blumen, das kleinste Haus.**
BUT **alt: der/die/das** *älteste*; **groß: der/die/das** *größte*

Those which add an **Umlaut** in the comparative keep it in the superlative:
e.g. **Die Windmühle ist Theos** *größtes* **Hobby.**

Superlatives can never be used without an ending; if the adjective is not in front of the noun you normally need to say **am . . .-en**:
e.g. **Die Spätlese schmeckt** *am besten*.

Irregular forms that you meet in *Deutsch direkt!* are:

gut **besser** **der/die/das** *beste*
hoch **höher** **der/die/das** *höchste*
nah **näher** **der/die/das** *nächste*
viel **mehr** **der/die/das** *meiste*

> Complete the sentences with the superlative form of the adjective:
>
> *a* Der Staatliche Hofkeller ist das (alt) _____ Weingut in Franken.
>
> *b* Dieses Hotel ist (billig) _____, aber es steht direkt am Bahnhof.
>
> *c* Die Brauerei zu Jever ist die (modern) _____ Brauerei in Ostfriesland.
>
> *d* Der (gut) _____ Wein ist die Spätlese, die (billig) _____ Sorte ist aber der Tafelwein.
>
> *e* Der (groß) _____ Weinkeller Frankens steht neben der Residenz zu Würzburg.
>
> *f* Die Männer machen die (schwer) _____ Arbeiten auf Sabine Langers Weingut.
>
> *g* Eine Weinprobe ist oft lustig; (lustig) _____ sind aber die Weinproben von Herrn Unger.

5 A relative pronoun links two parts of a sentence known as clauses:
e.g. I help young people   *who* have no job.
In German it is the appropriate form of **der, die, das**:
its gender and number depends on the word it 'relates' to
its case depends on whether it is the subject, object etc of the clause it introduces:
e.g. **Ich helfe Jugendlichen,** *die* **keine Arbeitsstelle haben.**

After a relative pronoun the verb goes to the end of that clause.

Fill in the gaps with **der, den, die** or **das**:

a Was ist der beste Wein, _____ Sie verkaufen?

b Wir machen hier recht lustige Weinproben, _____ sehr feucht-fröhlich sind.

c Heide hat einen Hund, _____ Wastl heißt.

d Sie hat eine Tochter, _____ das Gymnasium in Bremen besucht.

e Die Gäste, _____ nach Bad Mergentheim fahren, machen eine Kur.

f Die Patienten, _____ Gewichtsprobleme haben, dürfen keinen Kuchen essen.

g Das Wasser, _____ aus den Quellen in Bad Mergentheim kommt, schmeckt salzig.

h Die Touristen, _____ Richard durch Regensburg führt, kommen aus der ganzen Welt.

i Wir haben Probleme mit den Lehrern, _____ sehr schwer eine Anstellung finden.

Revision

6 The present tense of verbs

For details see the *Deutsch direkt!* course book page 299 ('regular' verbs),
page 300 (verbs with a vowel change in the singular), page 304 (separable verbs).

Select the appropriate verb from the list in the box and supply
the present tense of it:

a Wann _____ die Stadtführungen?

b Marion _____ abends bis halb zwölf.

c Ein Ausflug nach Walhalla _____ zwei Stunden.

d Herr Unger _____ Lebensmittel in seinen Geschäften.

e Richard Kerler _____ bald Lehrer.

f Bei Rot darf der Autofahrer nicht _____ .

g Um wieviel Uhr _____ du morgens?

h Petra _____ Marion im Café Lindau.

i Die Residenz zu Würzburg _____ dem Land Bayern.

j Der nächste Zug nach Berlin _____
     dreizehn Uhr.

k Sie müssen eine Tablette mit etwas Wasser _____ .

l Marions Mittagspause _____ nie, aber sie
     muß die Zeit nicht _____ .

m Christina _____ ihre Diät, denn sie
     _____ schnell.

abfahren
abnehmen
aufbleiben
aufstehen
ausreichen
dauern
durchhalten
einnehmen
gehören
nachholen
stattfinden
treffen
verkaufen
weiterfahren
werden

7 After **können** the verb goes to the end of that part of the sentence:
e.g. **Was kann man in Würzburg *machen*?**

Pair the verbs in the right-hand column with the appropriate activity, then continue the paragraph:

die Residenz und die Festung	_____	machen
Frankenwein	_____	besichtigen
eine Weinprobe	_____	trinken
ins Theater oder ins Kino	_____	spazierengehen
im Residenzgarten oder am Main	_____	gehen

In Würzburg kann man _____

Man kann _____

Man _____

_____

_____

8 How would you ask:

a Where is the bus stop? _____

b How do I get to Spetzerfehn? _____

c What's the best way to get to Würzburg? _____

d Where are the department stores? _____

e Where's the bus going to? _____

f Where is there a pharmacy near here? _____

Where are these people going?

g Komm Sebastian, wir gehen nach oben. _____

h Um wieviel Uhr fährst du nach Hause? _____

i Wie komme ich in die Stadt? _____

j Ilse fährt morgen in die Schweiz. _____

k Gehen Sie immer geradeaus! _____

l Die Post? Hier links um die Ecke. _____

11 *Was mögen Sie am liebsten?*

NEW WORD
schicken *to send*

---

1 **Dieser, diese, dieses** = *this*. The endings correspond to those of **der, die, das**.

Supply the correct version of **dieser**:

a Gehen Sie _____ Straße entlang.

b Wieviele Schüler hat _____ Gymnasium?

c Was kosten _____ Postkarten?

d Der Dom ist auf _____ Seite.

e Wie lange schon haben Sie _____ Hotel?

f _____ Äpfel sind sehr süß.

g Möchten Sie ein Stück von _____ Torte?

h Wie lange sind Sie schon in _____ Beruf tätig?

---

2 **Welcher, welche, welches** = *which*. The endings correspond to those of **der, die, das**.

i What was the question? Each one begins with **Welch . . .**

EXAMPLE *Welchen* **Wein trinkt Herr Langer am liebsten?**
Herr Langer trinkt den Silvaner am liebsten.

a _____ ? Wir nehmen diesen Wein.

b _____ ? Ich besuche die fünfte Klasse.

c _____ ? Dieses Brot schmeckt am besten.

d _____ ? Dieser Wein ist etwas billiger.

e _____ ? Die Patienten, die keine Gewichtsprobleme haben, dürfen Kuchen essen.

ii What was the question? Each begins with a preposition.

EXAMPLE *Mit welchem* **Zug fahren Sie?**
Wir fahren mit dem Intercity.

f _____ ? Von Gleis drei.

g _____ ? Ich habe im Juni Geburtstag.

h _____ ? Wir schließen am Mittwoch.

i _____ ? Wir möchten Karten für die Führung in englischer Sprache.

j _____ ? Sie arbeitet in Frankfurt.

3 The accusative case is used for the 'direct object' of a verb:
e.g. **Rolf hat** *einen Hund* **und** *eine Katze.*

The dative case is used for the 'indirect object':
e.g. **Er gibt** *seinem Hund* **ein Stück Fleisch und** *seiner Katze* **ein Stück Fisch.**
For details see pages 293–4 of the *Deutsch direkt!* course book.

Complete these sentences; decide whether the words in brackets should be in the accusative or dative case:

a Bringen Sie mir bitte (*an apple*) _____ .

b Jan Ole gibt (*his brother*) _____ eine Mark zehn.

c Darf ich Ihnen (*my wife*) _____ vorstellen?

d Moment, ich zeige (*the waitress*) _____ meinen Kuchenbon.

e Herr Unger bietet (*his customers*) _____ dreißig bis vierzig Sorten Wein.

f Nein! Du darfst (*the dog*) _____ keine Schokolade geben!

g Ich schicke (*my mother*) _____ (*a postcard*) _____ .

h Sebastian, gib (*your father*) _____ (*the sugar*) _____ .

4 Pronouns (**ich, mich, mir** etc) have different forms depending on how they are used in a sentence. They vary according to person, number, gender and case.
For details see pages 161 and 298 of the *Deutsch direkt!* course book.

Complete these sentences with the correct pronoun:

a Guten Tag, die Herrschaften. Was kann _____ für _____ tun? (*I/you*)

b Für die Langers ist die Weinlese die härteste Zeit im Jahr. _____ haben fast 24 Stunden Arbeit. (*they*)

c Entschuldigung, _____ suche die Post. Können Sie _____ helfen? (*I/me*)

d Frau Bender ist Sopran. _____ hat eine leichte, helle Stimme. (*she*)

e Der Volkacher Wein? Ich finde _____ ausgezeichnet! (*it*)

f Für meine Frau eine Tasse Kaffee und für _____ ein Kännchen. (*me*)

g Das mußt _____ _____ mal erklären, Jan Ole. Was ist WUK? (*you/to me*)

h Das zeige ich _____ hier auf dem Stadtplan. (*you*)

i Bringen Sie _____ bitte zwei Stück Schwarzwälder. (*us*)

5 When pointing to something you can say **das da!**, but if you've got its name in mind you should use the appropriate gender:
den da! (m) **die da!** (f) **das da!** (n)
To point to a number of things it's **die da!**

Reply to these questions as briefly as possible:

EXAMPLE **Möchtest du diese Postkarte?** *Nein, die da!*

a Möchten Sie diese Äpfel? Nein, _____ .

b Welchen Wein trinken Sie lieber? _____ .

c Sie nehmen dieses Brot hier, oder? Nein, _____ .

d Welche Blumen hätten Sie gerne? _____ .

e Was für Käse hätten Sie gern? _____ .

6 Possessives (**mein, dein, sein** etc) are determiners and add the same endings as are added to **ein** or **kein**.
For details see pages 294–5 of the *Deutsch direkt!* course book.

Complete these sentences with the correct form of the possessive:

EXAMPLE **Wie heißt denn *dein* Papa, Sebastian?**

a Was machst du in _____ Freizeit?   (*your*)

b Frau Bender ist Sopran; _____ Lieblingsrolle ist die Gretel.   (*her*)

c Wo sind _____ Weinberge, Herr Langer?   (*your*)

d Berthold Unger arbeitet in _____ beiden eigenen Geschäften.   (*his*)

e Wir haben in _____ Liste über hundert Sorten Wein.   (*our*)

f Ich habe einen VW Käfer, aber _____ Traumauto ist ein Sportwagen.   (*my*)

g Ich wohne zu Hause bei _____ Eltern.   (*my*)

h Geben Sie mir bitte _____ Kuchenbon.   (*your*)

i Die Steenblocks haben vier Kinder; _____ Kinder heißen Hajo,   (*their*)
   Johnny, Hilke und Nancy.

7 **Mögen** *to like*: both **ich mag** and **ich möchte** are derived from **mögen**.
Ich mag etc says what people *like*:
e.g. **Er *mag* gern Käsekuchen.** *He likes cheese cake.*
Ich möchte etc denotes what people *would* like:
e.g. **Er *möchte* gern Käsekuchen.** *He would like cheese cake.*
Both versions are set out on page 161 of the *Deutsch direkt!* course book.

Supply the correct version of **mögen**:

a Richard und Trudi _____ Lehrer werden.

b Was _____ du lieber, Englisch oder Mathe?

c Klassische Musik _____ Dr Weiß überhaupt nicht.

d Wir _____ bitte heute nachmittag eine Hafenrundfahrt machen.

e Mokkatorte _____ ich nicht so gern. Haben Sie Käsetorte?

f Frau Hadrian _____ sechs Briefmarken zu siebzig.

g Herrentorte? Das ist Schokoladensahne mit Weinbrand abgeschmeckt. _____
   Sie Weinbrand?

h Ich _____ bitte ein Kilo Äpfel.

8 When you're making a comparison:
so . . . wie: Die Himbeertorte ist nicht *so* süß *wie* die Herrentorte.
           – use **wie** after an 'ordinary' adjective
. . . -er als: Die Herrentorte ist süßer *als* die Himbeertorte.
           – use **als** after a comparative adjective
See Chapter 10, Exercise 3, for comparative adjectives.

Complete these sentences using whichever of the above forms makes better sense:

a Jan Ole hat WUK (gern) _____ _____ Mathe.

b Jan Ole schwimmt (schnell) _____ _____ die meisten Jungen in
   seiner Klasse.

c Er macht Rückenkraul nicht so (gern) _____ _____ Freistil.

d Die Tulpen kosten genau so (viel) _____ _____ die Rosen, zwei Mark das Stück.

e Die Pfirsiche sind (teuer) _____ _____ die Bananen.

f Mir schmeckt die Spätlese (gut) _____ _____ der Kabinett.

g Die Spätlese ist aber nicht so (süß) _____ _____ die Trockenbeerenauslese.

h Dieser Tafelwein ist noch (billig) _____ _____ ein Qualitätswein.

12 *Wo arbeiten Sie?*

NEW WORDS
der Hamster (-) *hamster*
die Maus (¨-e) *mouse*
die Himmelfahrt *Ascension Day*
der Maifeiertag *May Day holiday*
Pfingsten *Whitsuntide*

---

1 **gehören** *to belong*
The 'owner' generally goes into the dative case;
whatever they own is the subject, in the nominative case:
e.g. *Wem* (dat) **gehören** *die vielen Tiere* (nom)?

You're showing off the family photo album and have arrived at pets' corner. Explain to your German guest who all the animals belong to.

EXAMPLE **Der Vogel hier gehört** *meiner Großmutter.*   (*your grandmother*)

a Das ist unser Hamster. Er _____ .   (*your sister*)

b Diese Mäuse _____ .   (*your brother*)

c Die kleine Katze _____ .   (*your mother*)

d Die Goldfische _____ .   (*you*)

e Das ist unser Hund. Er _____ .   (*the whole family*)

---

2 There are three ways of expressing a liking for something:
add **gern/lieber/am liebsten** after the verb: **Jan Ole schwimmt** *gern.*
mögen, sometimes also with **gern** etc: **Alle Kinder** *mögen* **Eis.**
gefallen: **Mein Haus** *gefällt* **mir gut.**

gefallen   *to like, to please*
The person who is pleased generally goes into the dative case; whatever pleases them is the subject, in the nominative case:
e.g. *Seine Arbeit* (nom) **gefällt** *ihm* (dat) **gut.**

Choose the most appropriate expression from the box on the right to complete these sentences. Two must be used twice.

a _____ hier in Dinkelsbühl?

b _____ keinen Käse, oder?

c Was an seiner Arbeit _____ ihm so gut?

d Frau Wiemer _____ als Geschäftsführerin.

e Liebesfilme _____ Herrn Doktor Schwarz besser als Horrorfilme.

f Die Rosen im Residenzgarten _____ uns sehr.

g Die Arbeitszeit _____ mir nicht – ich möchte samstags gar nicht arbeiten.

h Unsere Lieblingsoper ist *Aïda.* Musicals _____ gar nicht.

i Frau Michaelis _____ Kaffee lieber als Tee.

mögen wir
gefällt
arbeitet gern
mag
gefallen
gefällt es Ihnen
du magst

3 In sentences where time (*when*) and place (*where*) are both mentioned, German normally places the time first:

e.g. **Arbeiten Sie** *das ganze Jahr hindurch* (*when*) **im Verkehrsamt** (*where*)?

Combine all the information into one sentence:

EXAMPLE **Heide Debus arbeitet in einer Schule.**
Seit wann?
Seit vier Jahren. *Heide Debus arbeitet seit vier Jahren in einer Schule.*

a Sebastian muß ins Bett.
Um wieviel Uhr?
Um Viertel nach acht. _____

b Heide möchte nach München fahren.
Heute schon?
Ja, heute nachmittag. _____

c Frau Bender singt im Stadttheater.
Wie oft?
Ungefähr dreimal in der Woche. _____

d Herr Langwisch arbeitet bei Bünting in Leer.
Wie lange?
Seit 17 Jahren. _____

e Ich fahre jetzt.
Wohin?
Nach Hause. _____

f Herr Haberland ist seit 22 Jahren Gärtner.
Wo?
Im Residenzgarten. _____

g Ein paar Gäste bleiben im Hotel.
Bis wann?
Bis Weihnachten. _____

h Michael hat morgen vormittag einen Termin.
Bei wem?
Bei Herrn Doktor Bergis. _____

---

4 There are two words for *when*, **wann** and **wenn**:

wann = *when?* is used in questions and 'implied' questions

e.g. *Wann* **melken Sie die Kühe?**
Ich weiß nicht, *wann* **der Bus kommt.**

wenn = *when, if, whenever* usually introduces a separate part of a sentence

e.g. *Wenn* **die Kunden unfreundlich sind, müssen wir Geduld haben.**

Fill each gap with the appropriate word:

a Seit _____ haben die Forckes ein Hotel in Dinkelsbühl?

b _____ Sie diese Straße entlanggehen, finden Sie ihn auf der rechten Seite.

c Bis _____ ist der Dom geöffnet?

d Herr Langwisch trinkt noch ein paar Tassen Tee, _____ abends Besuch kommt.

e _____ ist Ostersonntag?

f _____ er darf, möchte Richard in Regensburg arbeiten.

g Wissen Sie schon, _____ Sie zurückkommen?

5 When part of a sentence (a 'clause') begins with **wenn**, the verb comes at the end of that clause:

e.g. **Jan Ole geht nicht gern zur Schule,** *wenn* **er Englisch** *hat*.

Separable verbs do not split when they are at the end of a clause.
Compare: **Ich** *steige* **in München** *um*.
　　　　　Ich muß nur zehn Minuten warten, wenn ich in München *umsteige*.

If there is already an infinitive at the end, the other verb comes after it.
e.g. **Sie** *muß* **um zehn im Theater** *sein*.
　　　Frau Bender steht um neun Uhr auf, *wenn* **sie um zehn im Theater sein** *muß*.

Link the following pairs of sentences using **wenn**:

EXAMPLE **Frau Bender singt gern in Kirchen. Sie hat Zeit.**
　　　　　Frau Bender singt gern in Kirchen, *wenn* **sie Zeit** *hat*.

a　Nehmen Sie die Linie eins.　　　　Sie kommen aus dem Bahnhof.

b　Wir sind in fünf Minuten in der　　Wir fahren mit der Straßenbahn.
　　Stadt.

c　Es ist nicht schwer, eine Diät　　　Man sieht einen Erfolg.
　　durchzuhalten.

d　Ich darf Alkohol trinken.　　　　　Ich lasse etwas zum Essen weg.

e　Meine Arbeit ist frustrierend.　　　Ich kann einem Jugendlichen nicht helfen.

f　In Regensburg sind alle Hotels　　　Große Kongresse finden dort statt.
　　besetzt.

6 If the 'main clause' begins a sentence, the verb is the second element:
e.g. **Herr Langwisch** *trinkt* **noch mehr Tee, wenn abends Besuch kommt.**

If the main clause comes second, the whole 'wenn clause' becomes the first element:
e.g. **Wenn abends Besuch kommt,** *trinkt* **Herr Langwisch noch mehr Tee.**

Rewrite the sentences you constructed for Exercise 5, beginning each with the 'wenn clause'.

EXAMPLE *Wenn* **sie Zeit** *hat*, *singt* **Frau Bender gern in Kirchen.**

7 Ordinal numbers are normally formed by adding -**(s)te** to the cardinal number. For details see page 291 of the *Deutsch direkt!* course book.
Ordinal numbers are adjectives and have the usual adjective endings.

Using the calendar below in which only German public holidays are marked, answer the questions.

	MAI					JUNI			
So		6	13	20	27	3	10	17	24
Mo		7	14	21	28		4	11	18	25
Di	1	8	15	22	29		5	12	19	26
Mi	2	9	16	23	30		6	13	20	27
Do	3	10	17	24	31		7	14	21	28
Fr	4	11	18	25		1	8	15	22	29
Sa	5	12	19	26		2	9	16	23	30

EXAMPLE **Heiligabend ist** *am vierundzwanzigsten* **Dezember.**

a Wann ist der Maifeiertag in Deutschland?

Der Maifeiertag _____.

b In England ist der Maifeiertag der erste Montag im Mai.
Der wievielte ist das?
In England ist der Maifeiertag _____.

c Wann ist Himmelfahrt? (Das ist immer ein Donnerstag.)

Himmelfahrt _____.

EXAMPLE **Ostermontag ist** *der einunddreißigste* **März.**

d Der letzte Montag im Mai ist in Großbritannien ein Feiertag.
Der wievielte ist das?
Der letzte Montag im Mai _____.

e Pfingstsonntag ist dieses Jahr der erste Sonntag im Juni.
Der wievielte ist das?
Pfingstsonntag _____.

f Dieses Jahr ist der dritte Sonntag im Juni in Deutschland ein Feiertag.
Der wievielte ist das?
Der dritte Sonntag im Juni _____.

8 **Irgend-** gives a word or phrase a vague meaning:
e.g. **irgendwo** *somewhere, anywhere*
irgendwas *something or other, anything at all*

irgendwann	**irgendwo**	**irgendwie**
irgendwas	**irgendwohin**	**irgend jemand**

Fill the gaps, using each of the above words once:

_____ möchte ich sehr gern nach Japan fahren. Ich habe aber leider kein Geld. _____ muß ich in den nächsten Monaten Geld verdienen. Ich muß _____ Arbeit suchen. Hat _____ für mich eine Stelle? Was ich gern machen möchte? _____ ! Ich bin ja Mädchen für alles! Und wenn ich die Fahrt nach Japan nicht bezahlen kann, dann fahr' ich mit dem Rad _____ !

13 *Was machen Sie in Ihrer Freizeit?*

NEW WORD
gestern *yesterday*

---

1 When speaking to one child, close friend, relative etc the pronouns are:
du (nom)   **dich** (acc)   **dir** (dat)
If there's more than one, the pronouns are **ihr, euch, euch**

With **ihr** the verb ends in **-t**: e.g. **ihr wohnt, besucht, fahrt** etc *except* for **sein: ihr seid**

> You're talking to a group of children in Bamberg. Fill in the gaps with the correct pronoun or with the appropriate form of the verb:
>
> Wie (heißen) _____ du? Nun, Tobias, (kommen) _____ du aus Bamberg?
> Du auch, Tina? Nein? Woher (kommen) _____ du? Aus München, so. Es gefällt
> _____ allen hier in Bamberg, oder? Schön! Gefällt es _____ allen hier in
> Bamberg? Aber selbstverständlich, Bamberg ist ja eine schöne Stadt.
>   Na ja, was für Hobbys (haben) _____ ihr? Du Tina, du (spielen) _____
> Geige, und du Tobias, du (sich interessieren) _____ für Sport. (haben)
> _____ ihr Haustiere? Was! Drei Katzen! Süß!
>   Nun, Sonntag ist Erntedankfest. (gehen) _____ ihr in die Kirche? Was
> (machen) _____ du in der Kirche, Tina? Ah, du (müssen) _____ was
> vorlesen. Du auch, Tobias? Ihr (singen) _____ ja wahrscheinlich auch.
> (müssen) _____ ihr auch Obst aus dem Garten mitbringen? Die Kirche sieht
> bestimmt schön aus! Ich freue mich schon darauf.

---

2 Some verbs are 'reflexive', i.e. the subject and object are the same person or thing:
e.g. *Er hat sich erschossen. He* (subject) *shot himself* (object).

Note that German often needs a reflexive pronoun where you wouldn't always say '-*self*'
in English
e.g. *Susanne dreht sich um. Susanne turns (herself) round.*

The reflexive pronouns are set out on page 299 of the *Deutsch direkt!* course book.

> Complete the sentences using the verbs listed in the box; you will need one of
> them twice.

a Mein kleiner Bruder _____
   sehr für Musik.

b An der Ecke Hauptstraße Bahnhofstraße
   _____ eine Bank.

c Im Winter machen wir Hausarbeit, und wir
   _____ wieder auf das Frühjahr.

d Und dreißig Pfennig zurück. Ich _____ .
   Auf Wiedersehen.

e Herr und Frau Heß _____ besonders für Sport.

f Wenn ich _____ , sehe ich die Böttcherstraße
   und das Parlament.

g Du hast ja drei Geschwister – ihr _____ gut, oder?

h Erreiche ich eine Traumfigur? Ich _____ !

sich bedanken
sich befinden
sich bemühen
sich freuen
sich interessieren
sich umdrehen
sich verstehen

3 The normal way of saying what has been or used to be is to use the simple past of **sein**:
ich *war*, **du** *warst* etc.
Similarly you use the simple past of **haben**: **ich** *hatte*, **du** *hattest* etc.
Both verbs are set out in full on page 193 of the *Deutsch direkt!* course book.

Fill the gaps with the correct part of the appropriate verb:

a Frau Schretzenmayr _____ an der Nordsee.

b _____ du schon mal in England, Jan Ole?

c Bei der Weinlese _____ die Langers viel Arbeit.

d Andrea Wägerle _____ 1983 Weinkönigin von Franken.

e Wir _____ letzte Woche in Regensburg.

f Am Sonntag _____ ich Geburtstag.

g Sie möchten einen Termin bei Frau Doktor. _____ Sie schon einmal bei uns?

h Wo _____ Ihre Eltern dieses Jahr im Urlaub?

i Sie _____ ein Kännchen Kaffee und ein Stück Marzipankuchen, ja?

4 To form the perfect tense you need two elements:
the appropriate form of **haben** or **sein** (known as the 'auxiliary')
the 'past participle' of the verb, which comes at the end:
e.g. **Wir** *haben* **das Haus vor 12 Jahren** *gebaut.*
See page 193 of the *Deutsch direkt!* course book for more details.

Answer the questions using the information in brackets:

EXAMPLE **Welche Rolle haben Sie heute gesungen, Frau Bender?**
(die Adele in der *Fledermaus*)
Ich *habe* **heute die Adele in der** Fledermaus *gesungen.*

a Wo haben die Schretzenmayrs gewohnt?

Sie _____ . (in einem kleinen Hotel)

b Was für Tee haben wir getrunken?

Sie _____ . (Ostfriesentee)

c Welches Stück haben Sie gehört?

Wir _____ . (die Symphonie Nr 3 von
Ludwig van Beethoven)

d Wo hat Frau Michaelis gearbeitet?

Sie _____ . (im Garten)

e Was hast du dort gemacht?

Ich _____ . (eine Wanderung)

f Was hat Joachim gestern abend gesehen?

Gestern abend _____ . (eine halbe Folge von *Dallas*)

5 Most past participles are formed by putting **ge-** in front of the verb stem and adding **-t** (weak verbs) or **-en** (strong verbs).

Strong verbs often have a vowel change in the verb stem. You can check the vowel in the past participle by referring to the Glossary to *Deutsch direkt!*; it is the last of those listed, e.g. **trinken, a, u**

e.g. **In Würzburg haben wir einen sehr guten Wein** *getrunken.*

For more information see pages 301–2 of the *Deutsch direkt!* course book.

Transform these notes into sentences to produce an account of what everyone did this morning. Use the perfect tense; the 'auxiliary' you need is **haben**.

EXAMPLE **Stefanie   suchen   unsere Katze**
Stefanie hat unsere Katze gesucht

meine Eltern und dich	frühstücken	um 8 Uhr
Tina	spielen	Geige
Tante Leni und Onkel Bernd	machen	Gartenbeit
ich	lesen	eine Horrorgeschichte
Stefanie	finden	die Katze

6 Some perfect tenses are formed with **sein**. These include **sein** itself, **werden**, **bleiben** and most verbs indicating movement.

Lunch was quite eventful; continue the story you began in Exercise 5. Use the notes to write sentences in the perfect tense; take care to use the correct 'auxiliary'.

Papa	kommen	um halb eins nach Hause
wir	essen	zu Mittag
Onkel Bernd	trinken	zu viel Wein
er	gehen	ins Bett
er	schlafen	zwei Stunden
Mutti und Stefanie	fahren	zum Supermarkt
Tina und ich	bleiben	zu Hause

7 It is important not to confuse **werden** *to become* and **wollen** *to want to.*

werden   *to become*:   **Im Dezember** *wird* **Ilse 60.**
Wirst **du Lehrerin?**

NB **werden** often conveys a future sense.

wollen   *to want to*:   **Sebastian** *will* **auf den Stundenplan gucken.**
Er *will* **nicht ins Bett gehen.**

NB **wollen** conveys only what a person *wishes* to do, and nothing about what 'will' happen.

Both verbs are set out on page 191 of the *Deutsch direkt!* course book.

Fill in the gaps with the correct part of the appropriate verb:

a Wann _____ du zehn?

b Ich _____ in Regensburg arbeiten, aber ich habe noch keine Stelle gefunden.

c Ich möchte Musikerin _____ .

d Es gefällt mir nicht so gut, wenn die Touristen alles auf einmal wissen _____ .

e Gartenarbeit kann ein Hobby für mich _____ .

f Die Kurgäste _____ gesund _____ .

g _____ das Schloß nicht im Winter sehr kalt?

h Was _____ du später _____ ?

8 To say what you do or don't like doing, what you prefer and what you enjoy most of all, extend the verb by adding:

**nicht so gerne   (sehr) gerne   lieber   am (aller)liebsten
weniger gerne**

For a range of examples see page 160 of the *Deutsch direkt!* course book.

To talk about your favourite activity or object add **Lieblings-** to the beginning of the word e.g. **meine Lieblingsrolle**.

Complete the interview below with the most appropriate of the above expressions. Some must be used more than once.

Haben Sie ein Hobby?	Ja, ich lese _____ , ich singe _____ und ich höre _____ Musik.
Was machen Sie davon am liebsten?	Mein _____ hobby ist Musik hören.
Was für Musik hören Sie am liebsten?	_____ höre ich Operette, _____ die Operetten von Johann Strauß.
Haben Sie eine Lieblingsoperette?	Nein, ich höre fast alle seine Operetten _____ .
Hören Sie auch gern Oper?	Nein, Oper höre ich _____ , ich höre viel _____ Musicals.

14 *Wo wohnen Sie?*

1 Most past participles begin with **ge-** e.g. **gekommen, gesehen**.
Verbs which begin with **be-, emp-, ent-, er-, ge-, miß-, ver-, wider, zer-** or end in **-ieren**, never add **ge-** to the past participle:
e.g. **empfehlen**, *empfohlen*; **gehören**, *gehört*; **reservieren**, *reserviert*

Add the appropriate past participle:

a Wir haben das Schloß in den letzten Jahren _____ (renovieren).

b Wo hat es Ihnen am besten _____ (gefallen)?

c Hast du in Bremen den Dom _____ (besichtigen)?

d Die Steinhäusers haben auf dem Marktplatz _____ (protestieren).

e Tina hat _____ (erzählen), was sie am Sonntag in der Kirche machen muß.

f Was haben Sie heute _____ (fotografieren), Herr Kothe?

g Heute habe ich zwei Kleider und fünf Blusen _____ (verkaufen).

h Herr Kothe hat die Bilder selbst _____ (entwickeln) und _____ (vergrößern).

2 The past participles of separable verbs have **ge-** between the separable prefix and the rest of the verb.
e.g. **Die Postkarte ist erst gestern *angekommen*.**

These seven prefixes are always inseparable:
be-, emp-, ent-, er-, ge-, ver-, zer-

Add the appropriate past participle:

a Wir haben Baden-Baden _____ (besuchen).

b Christina Schistowski hat sehr stark _____ (zunehmen).

c Wieviel Kilo haben Sie schon _____ (verlieren)?

d In Bremen haben sie eine Hafenrundfahrt _____ (unternehmen).

e Seid ihr im Wald _____ (spazierengehen)?

f Ingrid und Uwe haben in Dinkelsbühl _____ (übernachten).

g Die Royal Air Force hat rund 90 Prozent der Stadt _____ (zerstören).

h Wann sind Sie aus dem Urlaub _____ (zurückkommen)?

i Berthold Unger ist mit Bier _____ (aufwachsen).

3 When a 'clause' begins with **weil** the verb comes at the end of it:
e.g. **Ich schwimme gern,** *weil* **ich einer der Schnellsten** *bin.*

If there is an 'auxiliary' verb (**haben**, **sein** in the past tense, **können**, **müssen** etc in the present tense), the auxiliary goes to the end:
e.g. **Ilse gefällt der Hochsommer nicht so sehr,** *weil* **die Touristen alles auf einmal** *wissen wollen.*
Compare: **Die Touristen** *wollen* **alles auf einmal** *wissen.*

Link the following pairs of sentences using **weil**:

EXAMPLE **Jan Ole hat Englisch nicht sehr gern. Der Lehrer ist doof.**
Jan Ole hat Englisch nicht sehr gern, *weil* **der Lehrer doof** *ist.*

a Angelika möchte in Würzburg arbeiten.   Ihr Mann ist in Würzburg berufstätig.

b Die Patienten trinken das Wasser.   Sie wollen gesund werden.

c Der Tourist bleibt nicht sehr lange in Würzburg.   Er ist auf der Durchfahrt nach Kassel.

d Wir sind gegen die neue Autobahn.   Sie zerstört den Wald.

e Tina muß jeden Tag Geige üben.   Sie will Musikerin werden.

f Richard Kerler führt Touristen durch Regensburg.   Er muß Geld verdienen.

g Sebastian muß sofort ins Bett.   Er hat am nächsten Tag zur ersten Stunde Unterricht.

h Frau Bender muß die jungen Mädchen spielen.   Sie hat eine leichte helle Stimme.

4 The 'passive' is used to say how things are done. It consists of the appropriate part of **werden** plus a past participle.
e.g. **Trotz allen Protesten** *wird* **die Autobahn** *gebaut.*

If you need to say *who* carries out the action of a passive verb it's **von**:
e.g. **Der Tee wird** *von Inge Ysker* (dat) **serviert.**
If the responsible agent is a *thing* it's **durch**:
e.g. **Unser Spaziergang wird** *durch die Autobahn* (acc) **unterbrochen.**

Answer the questions, using the passive:

EXAMPLE **Von wem wird das Brot für das Erntedankfest gebacken?** (Alfred Hoh)
Das Brot für das Erntedankest *wird* **von Alfred Hoh** *gebacken.*

a Was wird in der Oberen Pfarre gefeiert?
In _____ (das Erntedankfest)

b Welche Rollen werden von Heidemarie Bender gesungen?
Von _____ (die jungen Mädchen)

c Seit wann wird das Schloß renoviert?
Das _____ (seit etwa fünf Jahren)

d Von wem wird die deutsch-britische Gesellschaft geleitet?
Die _____ (Joachim Kothe)

e Wer wird medizinisch behandelt?
Alle Patienten _____

5 The object of an active verb becomes the subject of a passive verb.
e.g. **Ein Arzt leitet** *den Shanty-Chor.*
Der Shanty-Chor **wird von einem Arzt geleitet.**

If the 'agent' is mentioned, it's **von** for people, **durch** for things.

Rewrite in the passive:

EXAMPLE **Man exportiert den Wein in die ganze Welt.**
Der Wein wird **in die ganze Welt** *exportiert.*

a Man braut das Bier nach modernen Methoden. _____

b Man bäckt herrliches Brot aus dem Mehl. _____

c Die neue Autobahn zerstört den Wald. _____

d Der Staatliche Hofkeller produziert
eine Million Flaschen Wein. _____

e Die Frauen schneiden die Trauben und
die Männer tragen sie zum Wagen. _____

6 The object of an active verb becomes the subject of a passive verb.
e.g. **Im Schnoor verkauft man** *antiken Schmuck.*
Antiker Schmuck **wird im Schnoor verkauft.**

If the 'agent' is mentioned, it's **von** for people, **durch** for things.

Answer these questions using the passive:

EXAMPLE **Wer gibt die Musikkurse in Dinkelsbühl?**   (Sieglind Bruhn)
Die Musikkurse **in Dinkelsbühl** *werden von Sieglind Bruhn gegeben.*

a Wie oft melken Sie die Kühe?

_____   (zweimal am Tag)

b Zerstört man die schönen Häuser?

_____   (nein)

c Trinkt man viel Tee in Ostfriesland?

_____   (ja)

d Wer eröffnet das Volkacher Weinfest?

_____   (Andrea Wägerle)

e Produzieren Sie das Bier nach alten Methoden?

_____   (nach modernen Methoden)

f Wer leitet den Gymnastikkurs für Seniorinnen?

_____   (Ilse Wojaczek)

7 To find the meaning of an unfamiliar past participle you will need to identify the 'infinitive'. Verbs are always listed in the infinitive in dictionaries or the Glossary to *Deutsch direkt!*

List the infinitives of the past participles in these sentences:

a Ich habe eine halbe Folge von *Dallas* gesehen, das hat mir genügt.   _____

b Catherin hat ein Stück Himbeertorte und ein Glas Tee bestellt.   _____

c Ich bin verheiratet gewesen – meine gute Frau ist schon neun
Jahre tot.   _____

d Heute sind sie um fünf Uhr aufgestanden.   _____

e Mir hat es in England wunderbar gefallen.   _____

    f Herbert von Karajan hat Wagner nach Salzburg gebracht.   _____

    g Welchen Preis hast du heute gewonnen?   _____

    h Das Salzburger Hackbrett ist ein Instrument, das mein Vater
entwickelt hat.   _____

    i Der Bischof hat die Festung sehr viel ausgebaut und umgebaut.   _____

8 The 'genitive' case is used for several purposes including:
i to say *of the*
ii with the preposition **wegen**

In the genitive case proper names add **-s** without an apostrophe:
e.g. **auf den Straßen Bremens, Mozarts Kinder**

For more information see pages 293–4 of the *Deutsch direkt!* course book.

i   Complete the following phrases:

        EXAMPLE **in der Nähe** *des Rathauses*   *(the town hall)*

    a in der Nähe _____   *(a river)*

                _____   *(this forest)*

                _____   *(the shops)*

                _____   *(the church)*

    b am Rande _____   *(this town)*

                _____   *(the market place)*

                _____   *(a housing estate)*

                _____   *(the mountains)*

    c im Herzen _____   *(the village)*

                _____   *(Franconia* **Franken***)*

ii The preposition **wegen** can be used with either the genitive or dative, as the speaker
chooses.
When used with the genitive it sometimes comes after the noun:
e.g. **des Waldes wegen**

    Add the genitive on the left and the dative on the right:

    a _____   _____ *(the countryside)*

    b _____   _____ *(the child)*

    c _____ wegen _____ *(the tourists)*

    d _____   _____ *(my dog)*

15 Wie ist es?

1 The names of most towns can be used as adjectives by adding **-er**; there are no further changes. They are always written with a capital letter.
A few towns make 'unusual' adjectives: Bremen – **Bremer**; Jever – **Jever**

You've read about all these in *Deutsch direkt!* – or have you?
The list on the right has become jumbled; link each town to the appropriate object, then convert the name to an adjective.

EXAMPLE **der Hafen – Hamburg** = *der Hamburger Hafen*

a	die Residenz	Bad Mergentheim	_____
b	die Stadtmusikanten	Bamberg	_____
c	der Ratsherr	Berlin	_____
d	die Trinkkur	Würzburg	_____
e	das Bier	Dinkelsbühl	_____
f	der Dom*	Volkach	_____
g	die Symphoniker	Bremen	_____
h	der Nachtwächter	Regensburg	_____
i	die Philharmoniker	Jever	_____

* there are two possibilities for this one

2 The simple past of **wollen (ich *wollte*)** and **müssen (ich *mußte*)** are set out in full on page 222 of the *Deutsch direkt!* course book.

Similar verbs include **können** (ich *konnte*)
  dürfen (ich *durfte*)
  mögen (ich *mochte*)
  sollen (ich *sollte*)
You have already met **haben** (ich *hatte*)

Complete these statements about people you have met in *Deutsch direkt!* using the simple past:

a Richard Kerler und Trudi Lechner (wollen) _____ Lehrer werden.

b Tina Greiner (sollen) _____ jeden Tag Geige üben.

c Frau Schistowski (dürfen) _____ mal ein Stück Kuchen essen.

d Kurt und Angelika (können) _____ keine Arbeitsstelle finden.

e Marion Michaelis (haben) _____ einen uralten VW Käfer.

f Heidemarie Bender (müssen) _____ die jungen Mädchen spielen.

g Frau Hadrian (wollen) _____ keinen Videorekorder haben.

h Jan Ole (mögen) _____ Sport und Biologie lieber als Mathe und Englisch.

i Die Steenblocks (müssen) _____ die Windmühle renovieren.

j Sebastian (wollen) _____ aufbleiben, aber er (müssen) _____ um Viertel nach acht ins Bett.

3 More about the 'passive': to say how things *are* done use the present tense of **werden** with the 'past participle':
e.g. **Der Wein** *wird verkauft* **und** *exportiert.*

To say how things *were* done use the simple past of **werden** with the 'past participle':
e.g. **Die Straßen** *wurden* **nicht für Automobile** *gebaut.*
The simple past of **werden** is set out on page 223 of the *Deutsch direkt!* course book.

Complete these sentences using the appropriate tense of the 'passive' as illustrated above.

a Die Windmühle _____ vor vielen Jahren von Theo Steenblock und seiner Familie _____ .　(restaurieren)

b Frau Wiemers Garten _____ im Moment _____ .　(anlegen)

c Das Volkacher Weinfest _____ 1983 von Andrea Wägerle _____ .　(eröffnen)

d Zur Zeit _____ jährlich sehr viel Frankenwein _____ .　(exportieren)

e Nächste Woche _____ rund 400 Weine aus ganz Franken _____ .　(prüfen)

f Die schönen Brote, die Sie heute morgen in der Kirche gesehen haben, _____ von Herrn Hoh _____ .　(backen)

g Die Wurstküche _____ im 12. Jahrhundert _____ .　(bauen)

h Die Schutzgemeinschaft Alt-Bamberg paßt auf, daß die schönen alten Häuser nicht _____ _____ .　(zerstören)

4 You often see a preposition (e.g. **vor, aus**) with **da-** before it, **dar-** if the preposition begins with a vowel (e.g. **davor, daraus**).
It avoids the repetition of several words:
e.g. **Rechts von mir befindet sich eine Parfümerie.** *Daneben* (neben der Parfümerie) **ist das Bistro.**

Supply the missing word:

EXAMPLE **Wohnen Sie allein in Ihrem Haus? Ja,** *darin* **wohne ich allein mit meiner Frau.**

a Protestieren nur die Grünen gegen das Waldsterben?

Nein, ich bin kein Grüner und ich protestiere auch _____ .

b Die Garage befindet sich unter dem Haus.

_____ haben wir auch einen großen Keller mit einer Sauna.

c Joachim möchte wissen, was in Marions Garten wächst.

_____ wächst viel Unkraut, sagt sie!

d Was sieht man durch das Wohnzimmerfenster?

_____ sieht man leider den kranken Wald.

e Haben Sie etwas gegen Kopfschmerzen?

Ja, Aspirin ist gut _____ .

f Was halten Sie von einer Kur in Baden-Baden?

Ich halte gar nichts _____ .

g Interessierst du dich für Briefmarken?

Nein, aber mein Vater interessiert sich sehr _____ , er hat eine sehr schöne Sammlung.

h Der Baron lebt mit seiner Familie in einem alten Schloß.

_____ ist es im Winter sehr kalt.

i Freuen Sie sich auf Ihre Urlaubsreise?

Natürlich! Ich freue mich schon sehr _____ .

Revision

5 **an auf hinter in neben über unter vor zwischen**
can be followed by either the accusative or dative according to whether they answer the
question **wo** *where?* or **wohin** *where to?*

Supply the correct endings:

a Auf d____ Dach haben die Schistowskis einen Wetterhahn.

b Frau Wiemer möchte nicht wieder zurück in d____ Stadt.

c Dieses Jahr fahren wir an d____ Ostsee.

d Bei Rot dürfen Sie nicht über d____ Kreuzung fahren.

e Wir heißen Sie herzlich willkommen auf unser____ Schiff.

f Die Post befindet sich zwischen d____ Supermarkt und d____ Martinskirche.

g Ich gehe gern in d____ Wald spazieren.

h Die Langers verkaufen ihren Wein direkt an d____ Kunden.

i Sebastian guckt auf d____ Stundenplan.

j Man gießt den Tee über d____ Kandis.

k Frau Greiner ist Lehrerin an ein____ Gymnasium.

l Regensburg liegt an d____ nördlichst____ Punkt der Donau.

---

6   Complete these sentences by selecting the best verb from the list in the box and
using the present tense of it:

a Heide _____ in der Vorhalle des Bremer
Hauptbahnhofes.

b Der Ausgang _____ in Richtung Bahnhofsvorplatz.

c Bei der Bahnhofsauskunft _____ man Informationen.

d Wann _____ die Führungen?

e Eine Führung _____ normalerweise zwei Stunden.

f Die Touristen _____ den Regensburger Dom.

g Man _____ den Duft der historischen Wurstküche.

h Das Schiff _____ der Familie Klinger.

i Verkehrsprobleme _____ oft in älteren Städten.

j Die Wurstküche _____ jedes Jahr kilometerweise
Würstchen.

bekommen
riechen
besichtigen
vorkommen
gehören
sich befinden
dauern
herstellen
führen
stattfinden

---

7   Before attempting this exercise, look again at Chapter 5, Exercise 4 (adding **gern**
to a verb), Chapter 10, Exercises 3 and 4 (forming the comparative and
superlative), Chapter 11, Exercise 8 (comparisons using **wie** or **als**).

Theo Steenblock, whom you met in Chapter 6, has four children, Hajo, Johnny,
Hilke and Nancy. Ask him:

a Is Hilke younger than Hajo? _____

b Is Nancy the youngest? _____

c Who is the eldest? _____

d Does Hajo work better than Johnny? _____

e Do the children like helping with (**bei**) the work?_____

f Who most enjoys helping with the work? _____

8 Adjective endings vary according to the determiner they go with. When there is no determiner the endings are different again. Adjectives which are not immediately in front of the noun do not change.

For full details see pages 296–7 of the *Deutsch direkt!* course book.

Adjectives do not have capital letters unless:
i they are derived from place names, e.g. **die Bremer Stadtmusikanten**
ii they are part of a proper name, e.g. **die Steinerne Brücke**
das Alte Rathaus

Add the adjective endings in this 'mini tour' of Regensburg:

Regensburg hat eine 2000-jährig____ Geschichte. Im Mittelalter war die Stadt ein politisch____ und kirchlich____ Zentrum. Im Alt____ Rathaus tagte 1663 das erst____ deutsch____ Parlament. Der Regensburg____ Dom ist eine der wichtigst____ gotisch____ Kirchen in Deutschland. Interessant____ im Dom sind die viel____ bunt____ Glasfenster aus dem Mittelalter. Die berühmt____ Steinern____ Brücke ist fast 850 Jahre alt____ . Von der Brücke hat man einen schön____ Blick über die Stadt mit der Silhouette der viel____ Türme und Häuser. Riechen Sie den Duft der historisch____ Wurstküche? Die historisch____ Wurstküche ist berühmt____ für selbstgemacht____ Würstchen und für das selbstgemacht____ Sauerkraut. Die Würstchen schmecken einfach herrlich____ ! Heute nachmittag machen wir eine kurz____ Fahrt auf der romantisch____ blau____ Donau.

16 *Regensburg und Richtung Salzburg*

NEW WORD
der Stadtbummel (-)   *stroll through town*

---

1 Many words for jobs have different forms for men and women. The suffix **-in** is added to the feminine form, **-innen** to the feminine plural.

What job do they do? The jobs are listed in the box below in their masculine form.

a Helga Wiemer ist _____ in einem Laden für Damenoberbekleidung.

b Herr Waschek ist _____ . Seine Gemeinde ist nicht sehr groß.

c Barbara Haltenhof ist _____ im Arbeitsamt in Würzburg.

d Gerhard Herlyn ist _____ . Er hat 37 Kühe.

e Heidemarie Bender ist _____ am Stadttheater in Regensburg.

f Marion Michaelis arbeitet in einem Büro. Sie ist _____ .

g Herr Doktor Ketterer und seine Frau sind _____ in Bad Mergentheim.

h Hermann Feil stellt Barbara-Küsse und Regensburgerinnen her.
Er ist _____ .

i Dr Veit Löß sucht nach mittelalterlichen Funden. Er ist _____ .

j Herr Peithner stellt Kunstwerke aus Schmiedeeisen her. Er ist _____ .

k Catherin Debus und Dorle Adler gehen noch zur Schule. Sie sind _____ .

l Leo Langer und seine Frau sind _____ . Sie haben einen kleinen Weinberg in Volkach.

m Trudi Lechner ist _____ . Sie studiert Englisch und Kunsterziehung.

> Archäologe Arzt Berufsberater Geschäftsführer Kunstschmied Landwirt
> Opernsänger Pfarrer Pralinenmacher Schüler Sekretär Student Winzer

---

2 'Weak' and 'strong' verbs form their simple past in different ways. For details see pages 300–1 of the *Deutsch direkt!* course book.

Vowel changes in strong verbs are shown after the infinitive in the Glossary to *Deutsch direkt!* The change which applies to the simple past is always next to the end, e.g. **geben (i), a, e,** = **er/sie/es/man** *gab*.

Complete these sentences with the simple past of each verb:

a In der Nacht vom 16. auf den 17. März (stehen) _____ Würzburg in Flammen.

b Die Schilder zeigen, wo früher die Handwerker (wohnen) _____ .

c Der Dinkelsbühler Nachtwächter (machen) _____ seine Runde von der Abenddämmerung bis zur Morgendämmerung.

d Die Steinerne Brücke (verbinden) _____ die freie Reichsstadt Regensburg mit dem Land Bayern.

   e   Man (müssen) _____ Zoll zahlen, wenn man in die Stadt
       (wollen) _____ .

   f   Die Windmühle (sein) _____ eine Ruine, als Theo sie
       (kaufen) _____ .

   g   Regensburgs Lage am nördlichsten Punkt der Donau (geben) _____
       der Stadt historische Bedeutung.

   h   Links von dem Kaiser (sitzen) _____ die Kurfürsten.

   i   In alten Zeiten (müssen) _____ der Nachtwächter aufpassen, daß
       kein Feuer (ausbrechen) _____ .

3   The 'conditional' form of a verb expresses what *would be* or *would happen if* certain
conditions were fulfilled.
e.g. **Ich *würde* gern in der Industrie arbeiten. Das *wäre* schön.**
It also is a means of being particularly polite.
e.g. ***Würden* Sie sich bitte eintragen? Ich *möchte* gern Kaffee.**

The 'conditional' is formed by adding an **Umlaut** to the simple past of:
werden (ich *würde*)   **dürfen (ich *dürfte*)**   **können (ich *könnte*)**
mögen (ich *möchte*)   **müssen (ich *müßte*)**   **haben (ich *hätte*)** etc

As usual, **sein** is a law unto itself:

        ich *wäre*   **wir *wären***
         du *wärst*   **ihr *wärt***
er/sie/es/man *wäre*   **Sie/sie *wären***

   Fill the gaps with the 'conditional' form of the verb in brackets:

   a   Was (sein) _____ Ihr Traumauto?

   b   Ich (haben) _____ gern ein Stück Edamer.

   c   Ich (werden) _____ sagen, Salzburg ist eine der schönsten Städte
       der Erde.

   d   Hier bei Tomaselli (konnen) _____ Marcello stundenlang sitzen
       und zugucken.

   e   (werden) _____ Frau Fiedler Salzburg als Urlaubsort empfehlen?

   f   (mögen) _____ du deinen Brieffreund mal besuchen?

   g   Herr Reiser (werden) _____ gern Gitarre spielen, wenn er eine
       (haben) _____ .

   h   (werden) _____ Sie sich bitte eintragen?

   i   Man (können) _____ sagen, die Pralinen sind billig im Vergleich zur
       Industrieware.

   j   Wenn Sie Geschäftsführer (sein) _____ , (müssen) _____ Sie
       länger arbeiten.

Revision

4

Before tackling this exercise, look again at Chapter 10, Exercise 5.

Fill in the gaps with the relative pronoun:

EXAMPLE **Salzburg ist eine Stadt, *die* das ganze Jahr über Saison hat.**

a Wir heizen nur die Zimmer, _____ wir wirklich brauchen.

b Dieser Baum, _____ normalerweise im Sommer grün ist, hat die Blätter verloren.

c Es ist der sonnigste Platz, _____ Ilse hat.

d Woher kommen die Fische, _____ Sie fangen?

e Die Jugendlichen, _____ wir helfen, finden bald eine Stelle.

f Der neue Kanal verbindet den Main, _____ durch Würzburg fließt, mit der Donau.

g Sind Sie die einzige Familie hier, _____ Fische fängt und verkauft?

h Das Haus, _____ die Schistowskis seit 1980 bewohnen, ist ein Neubau.

i Was halten Sie von dem Tor, _____ Herr Peithner geschmiedet hat?

j Es gibt Monate, in _____ Frau Bender fünfzehn Vorstellungen hat.

5

The notebook below shows what you and your companion plan to do (**was Sie machen wollen**) on your forthcoming visit to Regensburg.

Complete the sentences to give an account of your plans:

EXAMPLE **Am ersten Abend *wollen wir* in der Altstadt einen Stadtbummel *machen*.**

The verbs you will need are listed below; some are needed more than once.

```
besichtigen   essen   fahren
gehen   machen   probieren   sehen
```

in der Altstadt: Stadtbummel

Mi. Stadtführung
    zus Walhalla (mit dem Schiff)
    die Fledermaus (Stadttheater)
Do. Karmelitengeist (im Kloster)
    Würstchen mit Sauerkraut
    (in der hist. Wurstküche !!!)
    Altes Rathaus
    Weinprobe bei Herrn Unger
Fr. Zum Fischmarkt (zu Fuß)
    – dann nach Hause

Mittwoch vormittag _____

Am Nachmittag _____

Mittwoch abend _____

Donnerstag vormittag _____

Zu Mittag _____

Nach dem Mittagessen _____

Am Abend _____

Am nächsten Morgen _____

Dann _____

6   Everything went according to plan.

Rewrite the account of the events which you prepared in Exercise 5 so that it describes what you actually did. Use the perfect tense:

EXAMPLE   **Am ersten Abend** *haben* **wir in der Altstadt einen Stadtbummel** *gemacht.*

7   Compare the following pairs like this:

EXAMPLE   **Der Eiffelturm**   **hoch**   **der Regensburger Dom**
           Der Eiffelturm ist *höher als* **der Regensburger Dom.**

a Regensburg	groß	Etterzhausen
b Februar	kurz	März
c Frau Peithner	jung	ihr Mann
d der Sommer	warm	der Winter
e Andreas Festkleid	lang	ihre normalen Kleider
f die Bahnhofsgaststätte	teuer	das Bistro

17   *Altstadt*

---

1 To form the future tense use the present tense of **werden** with the 'infinitive', which goes to the end of the 'clause'.

e.g. **Im Urlaub** *werde* **ich wahrscheinlich in die Schweiz** *fahren.*

Note that the future tense is less common in German than in English (see Chapter 13, Exercise 7).

Answer the questions, incorporating the information in brackets:

EXAMPLE **Werden Sie das Schloß renovieren?**   (von außen)
Wir werden **das Schloß von außen** *renovieren.*

a Wie viele Studenten werden in diesem Haus wohnen?

   In diesem Haus _____ (neunzig Studenten)

b Wo werden Sie protestieren?

   Wir _____ (vor dem Parlament in Bremen)

c Was wird Dorle Adler studieren?

   Sie _____ (Englisch und Geschichte)

d Wann wird Joachim die Bilder vergrößern?

   Er _____ (heute abend)

e Was wirst du in Salzburg besichtigen?

   Ich _____ (Mozarts Geburtshaus und die Festung)

---

2 **Um . . . zu** is used to express a purpose; an infinitive completes the phrase. Phrases with **um . . . zu** are separated from the rest of the sentence by a comma:

e.g. **Ich mache Stadtführungen,** *um* **mir als Student Geld** *zu verdienen.*

Combine the following sentences with **um . . . zu.**

EXAMPLE **Gerhard Herlyn muß früh aufstehen. Er melkt die Kühe.**
Gerhard Herlyn muß früh aufstehen, *um* **die Kühe** *zu melken.*

a Ich gehe auf den Markt.   Ich kaufe Blumen und Gemüse.

b Frau Wiemer fährt mittags nach Hause.   Sie ißt Joghurt und Obst.

c Fünfzigtausend Gäste kommen jedes Jahr nach   Sie machen eine Kur.
   Bad Mergentheim.

d Wir brauchen acht bis zehn Wochen.   Wir brauen ein gutes Bier.

e Die Touristen kommen abends aus ihren   Sie machen einen kleinen
   Zimmern heraus.   Stadtbummel.

f Katrin fährt nach Würzburg.   Sie besichtigt die Residenz und
                                                  den Rosengarten.

g Die Steinhäusers sind nach Bamberg gegangen.   Sie haben auf dem Marktplatz
                                                  protestiert.

Revision

3   How good are your numbers?

You have been asking lots of questions, but the answers have become jumbled.
Match the correct answer to each question:

a	Haben Sie einen großen Garten?	Etwa 15 Kilometer.
b	Wieviele Pralinen verkaufen Sie im Jahr?	Zirka 150.000 Fläschchen im Jahr.
c	Und wieviel möchten Sie von dem Ostfriesentee?	Grob gerechnet etwa 5.000 Kilogramm.
d	Wieviel verkaufen Sie von dem Karmelitengeist?	An die tausend Quadratmeter.
e	Was macht das zusammen?	50 Pfennig das Stück.
f	Wo in der Getreidegasse wurde Mozart geboren?	Hundert Gramm.
g	Wieviele Unterschrifte haben Sie gesammelt?	OHZ-TE 66.
h	Wie weit ist Etterzhausen von hier?	Sie ist 310 Meter lang.
i	Wie lange mußt du üben?	Seit 16 Jahren.
j	Ist die Steinerne Brücke sehr klein?	Es hat ungefähr 150 Quadratmeter Wohnfläche.
k	Wie lange wohnen Sie hier draußen?	Eine halbe Stunde.
l	Was kosten die Eier?	Ungefähr 4.000 Stück.
m	Wie groß ist das Haus?	Zehn Mark und zwanzig.
n	Sie haben einen Ford, ja? Mit welcher Nummer?	In der Nummer neun.

4   Supply the appropriate question words from the box on the right.
Take care – there's one too many!

a _____ kommen die Fische, die Sie fangen?

b _____ stellt das Kloster den Karmelitengeist her?

c _____ können Sie Ihrem Mann helfen, Frau Peithner?

d _____ Pralinen verkaufen Sie im Jahr?

e _____ sind die Pralinen so teuer?

f _____ zeigen Sie bei einer Führung, Frau Unger?

g _____ hat Ihre Ausbildung gedauert?

h _____ malt auf dem Alten Markt Porträts?

i _____ in der Getreidegasse wurde Mozart geboren?

j _____ Qualitäten brauchen die Schüler in der Mittenwalder Geigenbauschule?

k _____ begann die Restaurierung des Regensburger Doms?

seit wann
wann
warum
was
welche
wer
wie
wie lange
wieviele
wo
woher
wohin

5 Words form their plurals in a variety of ways. A few plurals are totally unexpected. It is advisable to learn each one as you come across it.

Give the plurals of:

der Fluß _____   der Kaufmann _____

der Baum _____   das Restaurant _____

das Blatt _____   das Sanatorium _____

der Domturm _____   das Hobby _____

das Zentrum _____   der Ordensbruder _____

das Shanty _____   die Prüfung _____

das Erzeugnis _____   die Regensburgerin _____

das Gymnasium _____   der Chef _____

der Stock _____   der Bau _____

6 If you're saying where or when something originated it's *aus* (plus dative):
e.g. **Herr Peithner kommt *aus* Karlsbad. Die Mühle ist *aus dem* 19. Jahrhundert.**

Match each object to its correct origin, and complete the sentences, using part of **kommen**:

EXAMPLE **Mozart *kommt aus Salzburg.***

a Der saure Regen _____ (die ganze Welt)

b Einige Zutaten für den Karmelitengeist _____ (eine Zeitschrift)

_____

c Die Fische, die die Hofmeisters verkaufen, _____ (der Garten des

_____ Karmelitenklosters)

d Die Touristen, die nach Rothenburg kommen, _____ (die Industriegebiete)

e Frau Schistowskis Diät _____ (die Donau)

_____

7 You can't improve on these – they're the biggest and best of their kind!

EXAMPLE **Die Getreidegasse ist _____ (bekannt) _____ Straße Salzburgs.**
Die Getreidegasse ist *die bekannteste* Straße Salzburgs.

a Die Steinerne Brücke ist _____ (alt) _____ Steinbrücke in Deutschland.

b Das Weinfest in Volkach ist _____ (groß) _____ und (schön) _____ in ganz Franken.

c _____ (viel) _____ Touristen bleiben nicht sehr lange in Rothenburg.

d Düsseldorf ist vielleicht _____ (elegant) _____ Stadt in Deutschland.

e Bei der Prämierung bekommen _____ (gut) _____ Weine eine Goldmedaille.

f Salzburg ist eine _____ (schön) _____ Städte der Erde.

g Die Winds haben _____ (klein) _____ Haus von ganz Österreich.

h Für die Winzer ist die Weinlese _____ (wichtig) _____ und (hart) _____ Zeit im Jahr.

i Die Strudelrundfahrt ist _____ (beliebt) _____ Route.

8   Select whichever of the two verbs you feel is more appropriate to the sense and supply the correct form of it:

a   Herr Feil probiert die Pralinen, die er herstellt.

   Er _____ seine Pralinen sehr gern.   (müssen/mögen)

b   Die Zutaten für das Feuerwasser sind ein Geheimnis.

   Pater Wilfried _____ nicht sagen, was drin ist.   (dürfen/müssen)

c   Arbeiten die Steinmetzen nur in der Dombauhütte?

   Nein, sie _____ direkt an der Fassade des Doms   (mögen/müssen)
   arbeiten.

d   Frau Wind hat das kleinste Geschäft in Salzburg.

   Ein größeres Geschäft _____ sie aber nicht haben.   (wollen/dürfen)

e   In dem Salzburger Marionettentheater _____ das   (wollen/sollen)
   Publikum den Eindruck bekommen, daß die Puppen leben.

f   Wo bekommt man Karmelitengeist?

   Man _____ ihn in Apotheken in ganz Süddeutschland   (mögen/können)
   kaufen.

18 *Fasching und Festspiele*

NEW WORD
per Anhalter fahren   *to hitchhike*

---

1   Where two nouns mean the same thing, they are in the same case:
e.g. **Ich wohne in** *Oberneuland* (dat), *einem Stadtteil* (dat) **von Bremen.**

Fill the gaps with the correct endings:

a Sonntag früh in Spetzerfehn, ein____ klein____ Dorf in Ostfriesland.

b Ich besitze einen Volkswagenbus, ein____ alt____ Campingbus.

c Das Dirndl von Andrea Wägerle, d____ jung____ Weinkönigin von Volkach, ist aus Seide und Brokat.

d Der Garten gehört zur Residenz, d____ herrlich____ Würzburger Barockschloß.

e Dann gibt es eine Neuinszenierung von *Jedermann*, d____ Herzstück der Salzburger Festspiele.

f Hofmannsthal hat die Vorlage von *Everyman* verwendet, ein____ englisch____ Mysterienspiel.

g Constanze liegt in Salzburg begraben, zusammen mit Leopold, d____ Vater Mozarts.

h Die Osterfestspiele sind eine Kreation Herbert von Karajans, d____ berühmt____ Dirigenten.

i Salzburg liegt zwischen zwei Bergen, d____ Mönchsberg und d____ Kapuzinerberg.

---

2   In German word order *when* (time) normally comes before *how* (manner). Both *when* and *how* normally come before *where* (place).
e.g. **Das ist** *etwa zehn Minuten* (when) *mit dem Auto* (how) *von der Innenstadt entfernt* (where).

Before tackling this exercise look again at Chapter 7, Exercise 6; Chapter 8, Exercise 2; and Chapter 12, Exercise 3.

i   Your family has a bad attack of wanderlust this summer. Write a sentence about each person to explain to your German friends where they are all off to.

EXAMPLE *18.2 James – Mayrhofen by train*
        James fährt am achtzehnten Februar mit dem Zug nach Mayrhofen.

26.5 Sandy and wife – Switzerland by car _____

 9.6 Tracy – hitchhiking to Spain _____

16.6 Uncle Peter and Aunt Helen – USA by boat _____

 7.7 you yourself – Salzburg by bus _____

31.7 your parents – Turkey by rail _____

ii   Now rewrite your answers, beginning with the 'time' phrase:

EXAMPLE **Am achtzehnten Februar** *fährt James* **mit dem Zug nach Mayrhofen.**

_____

_____

_____

_____

_____

3 A small group of nouns add **-n** or **-en** in all cases in the singular except nominative. Those you meet in *Deutsch direkt!* include:

Geselle Herr Junge Kollege Komponist Steinmetz Straßenmusikant Student

Complete these sentences with the word in brackets, adding an ending if necessary:

a Als Meister hat Herr Maller jetzt selbst einen _____ .   (*apprentice*)

b Für einen _____ ist es leicht, Geld zu verdienen.   (*student*)

c Mein _____ und ich fahren nach Salzburg.   (*colleague*)

d Martin, der Sohn von _____ Brütt, macht das Futter für die Pferde.   (*Mr*)

e Für einen _____ ist Paddeln ein schönes Hobby.   (*boy*)

f Das ist für einen _____ eine wirklich große Aufgabe.   (*stonemason*)

g Ein deutscher _____ muß das Studium selbst bezahlen.   (*student*)

h Das Maskenschnitzen macht _____ Angele hobbymäßig seit 20 Jahren.   (*Mr*)

i Diese Geige ist von Max Rüst, dem _____ von _____ Maller.   (*apprentice*) (*Mr*)

j Ein _____ muß sein Handwerk erlernen.   (*stonemason*)

k Meine Geigen kosten sechstausend Mark, die meines _____ kosten die Hälfte.   (*apprentice*)

l Die Salzburger Festspiele wurden von einem berühmten _____ gegründet.   (*composer*)

Revision

4   Verbs: See pages 299–305 of the *Deutsch direkt!* course book.

i   The present tense, including separable, inseparable and reflexive verbs.
Complete these sentences using the present tense of the verb in brackets:

  a In Mittenwald _____ (austreiben) die Schellenrührer den Winter

  b Die neue Autobahn _____ (unterbrechen) unseren Spaziergang

  c Herr Maller _____ (auswählen) immer selbst das Holz

  d Dorle und ihre Geschwister _____ (sich verstehen) gut

  e Die Universität Regensburg _____ (errichten)
Studentenwohnungen in der Altstadt

  f Die Studenten _____ (zusammensitzen) im Gemeinschaftsraum

  g Wir _____ (sich interessieren) nicht für neue Musik

  h Die Grünen _____ (sich beschäftigen) mit Umweltproblemen

  i Ich _____ (sich freuen) auf das Erntedankfest

  j Wir _____ (spazierengehen) sehr oft im Wald

ii   The perfect tense:
Rewrite sentences *e*, *i* and *j* in the perfect tense.

  e _____

  i _____

  j _____

iii   The passive:
Rewrite sentences *a*, *b* and *e* in the passive – use the present tense of **werden**.

  a _____

  b _____

  e _____

iv   The future:
Rewrite sentences *b*, *f* and *h* in the future tense.

  b _____

  f _____

  h _____

v   Modal verbs:
Rewrite sentences *a*, *f* and *j* incorporating the present tense of **wollen**, **dürfen** and
können respectively.

  a _____

  f _____

  j _____

5 Expressions of time

Answer the questions fully, using the information given in brackets:

EXAMPLE **Wann hat Salzburg Saison?**   (*the whole year round*)
Salzburg hat *das ganze Jahr über* Saison.

a Wie lange schläft der Bäckermeister am Nachmittag?

Am Nachmittag _____ (*for three hours*)

b Wie lange wohnen Sie schon in Regensburg, Frau Peither?

Wir _____ (*for 40 years*)

c Wann findet die Premiere statt?

_____ (*on 29 July at 5 pm*)

d Wie lange könnte Marcello sitzen und zugucken?

_____ (*for hours*)

e Wie oft finden die Stadtführungen statt?

_____ (*twice a day*)

f Wann hat die Wurstküche Ruhetag?

Ruhetag _____ (*once a year; at Christmas*)

g Wie lange dauert die Ausbildung eines Kunstschmiedes?

_____ (*eleven years*)

h Wann begann die Restaurierung des Regensburger Doms?

_____ (*a hundred years ago*)

i Wann kann man das Schellenrühren sehen?

Das Schellenrühren _____ (*on 'mad Thursday'*)

j Wie lange dauern die Sommerfestspiele?

_____ (*from the end of July
to the end of August*)

---

6 When a clause begins with **wenn** the verb goes to the end.
In a main clause the verb is always the second element; the first element may be one word, a group of words or even a whole clause.

Match each of the sentences on the right with the most appropriate one from the left-hand column.
Join each pair, using **wenn** with the 'clause' from the left-hand column.

EXAMPLE **Es muß sein. Pater Wilfried trinkt Karmelitengeist.**
Wenn es sein *muß*, *trinkt* Pater Wilfried Karmelitengeist.

a Man hat es eilig.	Sie malen ein Kreuz darauf.
b Man geht über die Steinerne Brücke.	Frau Bender muß eine Stunde vorher im Theater sein.
c Sie hat eine Vorstellung.	Sie brauchen Hotelzimmer.
d Er hat zur ersten Stunde Unterricht.	Im Bistro kann man schnell Würstchen und Kartoffelsalat zu sich nehmen.
e Man hat Glück.	Man hat einen schönen Blick über die Stadt.
f Die Grünen finden einen kranken Baum.	Sebastian muß früh ins Bett.
g Die Touristen kommen in Regensburg an.	Man bekommt Karten für die Festspiele.

7   The genitive case

Before tackling this exercise look again at Chapter 9, Exercise 5 and Chapter 14, Exercise 8.

Complete these sentences by adding the genitive case of the words in brackets:

EXAMPLE   *Jedermann* **ist das Herzstück** _____ (die Salzburger Festspiele)

Jedermann **ist das Herzstück** *der Salzburger Festspiele.*

a   Durch den Lärm _____ (die Schellen) wird der Winter ausgetrieben.

b   Die Mittenwalder Holzmaske ist das Gesicht _____ (ein junger Mann).

c   Wir haben die Städte am Rande _____ (der Schwarzwald) besichtigt.

d   In Rothenburg sind die Fassaden _____ (die alten Häuser) noch gut erhalten.

e   Der Pfarrer _____ (diese evangelische Kirche) ist Wilfried Waschek.

f   _____ (Tina) Katzen heißen Mollis, Minka und Mucki.

g   Wir wohnen in der Nähe _____ (ein kleiner Fluß).

h   In Regensburg haben die Archäologen viele Gegenstände _____ (das tägliche Leben) gefunden.

i   Shantys sind die Arbeitslieder _____ (die alten Seeleute).

j   Mozart hat an den großen Höfen _____ (Europa) gespielt.

k   Heide ist in der Vorhalle _____ (der Bremer Hauptbahnhof).

l   Die Wurstküche wurde für die Bauleute _____ (die Steinerne Brücke) gebaut.

m   Die Osterfestspiele sind eine Kreation _____ (Herbert von Karajan).

19 *Schnee und Kaffee*

---

1 In 'subordinate' clauses the verb goes to the end.
In the future and perfect tenses and the passive, where verbs consist of two parts, the 'auxiliary' verb comes last.
e.g. **Bei der Prüfung werden 12 ausgewählt, die dann *aufgenommen werden*.**

Match these jumbled pairs of sentences, then link them using **wo**:

EXAMPLE **Von der Festung sehen Sie schön die Getreidegasse.   Dort wurde Mozart in der Nummer neun geboren.**
Von der Festung sehen Sie schön die Getreidegasse, *wo* Mozart in der Nummer neun *geboren wurde*.

a	In Jever gibt es eine Brauerei.	Dort haben wir die Residenz und die Festung besichtigt.
b	Die Wurstküche ist ein altes Restaurant.	Dort wurde 1816 *Stille Nacht* geschrieben.
c	Wir waren ein paar Tage in Würzburg.	Dort haben sie gegen die neue Autobahn protestiert.
d	Die Universität Regensburg baut Studentenwohnheime in der Altstadt.	Dort werden 30 bis 40 Sorten Wein probiert.
e	Das Café Mozart ist ein typisches Wiener Café.	Dort kann man herrliche Würstchen mit hausgemachtem Senf essen.
f	Bei Berthold Unger finden Weinproben statt.	Dort kann man Zeitung lesen.
g	Zwanzig Kilometer von Salzburg liegt Oberndorf.	Dort werden etwa 90 Studenten wohnen.
h	Die Steinhäusers und ihre Kinder sind nach Bamberg gegangen.	Dort wird das Bier nach ganz modernen Methoden gebraut.

---

2 Many verbs can be used as nouns; they are written with a capital letter and are always neuter:
e.g. **das Lesen** *reading*, **das Schlittschuhlaufen** *skating*, **das Autofahren** *driving*

Fill the gaps with the appropriate noun:

a (Skiing) _____ hat auch ein Geheimnis. Es ist so wie (swimming) _____ oder (cycling) _____ – man verlernt es nicht mehr.

b Lucki Rieser mag (hang-gliding) _____ sehr gern. Er sieht die Alpenlandschaft wie aus den Augen eines Vogels.

c (carving wooden masks) _____ hat in Mittenwald eine lange Tradition.

d (Ski-jumping) _____ war lange Zeit das Hobby von Engelbert Kroll.

e Beim Schellenrühren spielt (beer-drinking) _____ eine große Rolle.

f Für Roland Techet ist (playing the piano) _____ mehr als ein Hobby.

3   After **als, bevor, bis, damit, daß, weil, wenn, wo** etc the verb goes to the end of the clause (see Exercise 1, above).

After **aber, denn, oder, sondern, und** the verb is the second element.
e.g. **Mein Name ist Heinz Plöbst, aber hier *nennt* man mich Herr Heinz.**

Sort these jumbled sentences, adjusting the word order in your final version if necessary. The first one has been done for you.

a   Die Festspiele kann man nicht besuchen, weil [die Studenten auch in einer Gruppe zusammensitzen können].
Die Festspiele kann man nicht besuchen, weil *es keine Karten für Normalsterbliche gibt*.

b   Ich muß viel Wein trinken, aber [es schmeckt nicht gut].

c   Ich versuche in die Festspiele zu gehen, wenn [sie mit dem Schach fertig sind].

d   Die Schutzgemeinschaft Alt-Bamberg paßt auf, daß [dieser Garten sehr groß ist].

e   Für jedes Wohnheim gibt es einen Gemeinschaftsraum, so daß [er zum letzten Mal gesprungen ist].

f   Es gibt im Residenzgarten genug Arbeit für zwölf Gärtner, denn [wir brauchen den Wald zum Leben].

g   Das Wasser von der Quelle ist gesund, aber [es gibt keine Karten für Normalsterbliche].

h   Unsere Stammgäste bleiben länger sitzen, bis [ich einen Stehplatz bekommen kann].

i   Es ist sehr schlimm, daß die Bäume sterben, denn [ich trinke auch gerne viel Wein].

j   Es ist heute für Herrn Kroll ein besonderer Sieg, denn [die wertvollen Häuser werden nicht zerstört].

Revision

4   Supply the correct preposition, and where appropriate the determiner or ending. The prepositions you need are listed here:
auf   aus   bei   für   in   nach   von   wegen   zu

a   Dieses Geländer wurde _____ mein____ Mann angefertigt.

b   Sind Sie _____ erst____ Mal in Salzburg?

c   Die Steinerne Brücke wurde _____ 12. Jahrhundert gebaut.

d   Die Würstchen werden _____ Schweinefleisch hergestellt.

e   _____ dies____ schön____ Wetter benutzt fast niemand ein Auto.

f   Die Wurstküche ist berühmt _____ selbstgemacht____ Würstchen.

g   Eben d____ Wald____ _____ wohnen wir so gerne hier.

h   Ich möchte bitte einen Termin _____ Herr____ Doktor Salzer.

i   Geben Sie mir bitte sechs Briefmarken _____ ein____ Mark.

j   Wie können Sie Ihrem Mann _____ d____ Arbeit helfen, Frau Peithner?

k   Sind Sie in Salzburg _____ Urlaub?

l   Grüne Bohnen heißen _____ uns Fisolen.

m   Wir haben _____ Ostern die Osterfestspiele.

n   *Hänsel und Gretel* ist eine Oper _____ Engelbert Humperdinck.

o   Komm! Wir gehen schnell _____ Hause.

5 **Werden** is a 'maid-of-all-work' (see page 303 of the *Deutsch direkt!* course book).

How would you say:

a   When will you be ten? _____

b   How many students will live here? _____

c   Tina wants to be a musician. _____

d   Where is *Jedermann* performed? _____

e   The ski school was founded by Riki Spieß. _____

f   I'll soon be 76. _____

g   Twelve pupils are chosen. _____

h   I'll order it tomorrow. _____

i   Salzburg became too small for Mozart. _____

6   Saying what things are made of

Something's wrong here! All the substances except one are matched with the wrong item. Fill in the missing endings, then unscramble these sentences:

a   In Jever braut man Bier [_____ den edelst____ Rohstoff____].

b   Silvia Kirsch macht Schmuck [_____ Schweinefleisch].

c   Der Teufel und seine Großmutter sind Figuren [_____ Stein].

d   Andrea Wägerles Dirndlkleid ist [_____ drei verschieden____ Holzart____].

e   Die Würstchen in der Wurstküche sind [_____ Schmiedeeisen].

f   Eine Geige ist [_____ Glas].

g   Die Pralinen werden [_____ d____ Mehl] hergestellt.

h   [_____ Hopfen, Gerste und Wasser] wird herrliches Brot gebacken.

i   Herr Peithner ist Kunstschmied. Er stellt Kunstwerke [_____ Seide und Brokat] her.

7   These fourteen adjectives have been omitted from the passage below.
Rewrite the passage, using the adjectives in the order in which they are listed to describe an appropriate noun.
Check that the endings are correct and that the passage makes sense:

kleine   weltbekannten   verschiedenen   Mittenwalder   vielen   traditionelle jungen   bunten   berühmte*   jungen   kalten   kurze   weißes   sehr viel
* two possibilities for this one!

Mittenwald ist eine Stadt in Bayern. Dort ist der Geigenbau zu Hause. Qualitätsinstrumente werden in der Geigenbauschule gebaut. Eine Geige ist aus drei Holzarten. Auch aus Holz sind die Holzmasken, die hobbymäßig von Geigenbauern geschnitzt werden. Die Holzmaske ist das Gesicht eines Mannes. Man trägt diese Maske mit einem Kostüm zum Fasching. Eine Faschingstradition in Mittenwald ist das Schellenrühren am Unsinnigen Donnerstag. Durch den Lärm der Schellen wollen die Männer den Winter vertreiben. Die Schellenrührer tragen eine Lederhose, ein Hemd und eine Holzmaske. Sie ziehen von Gaststätte zu Gaststätte und trinken dabei Bier.

8   Rewrite these sentences and questions in the perfect tense. For information about the perfect tense see page 301 of the *Deutsch direkt!* course book.

a Ich studiere in Innsbruck Sport. _____

b In Bamberg sterben viele Bäume. _____

c Jan Ole hat Mathe und Englisch nicht so gern. _____

d Wir sind im Café Mozart in der Salzburger Getreidegasse. _____

e Frau Schretzenmayr fährt dieses Jahr in den Schwarzwald. _____

f Wie weit springst du, Robert? _____

g Werden Sie das Kostüm anprobieren? _____

h Wieviele Wohnungen werden Sie in der Stadt bauen? _____

i Was machen Sie, um Geld zu verdienen? _____

20 *Salzburg – ein letzter Besuch*

1   Word order

Put the boxes in the right order; do not change the order of words within each box:

a
- eine Stunde vor dem Schlafengehen
- einnehmen
- mit etwas Wasser
- Sie müssen eine Tablette

b
- zu Fuß
- nach Dinkelsbühl
- nach dem Krieg
- Sepp Laugner kam

c
- von der Innenstadt entfernt
- etwa zehn Minuten
- meine neue Wohnung liegt
- mit dem Auto

d
- gestern abend
- den Pfandlrostbraten hat
- Frau Unger
- bestellt
- im Café Mozart

e
- ungefähr seit 1945
- auf der Donau
- fährt meine Familie

f
- drei Jahre
- bei einem Meister
- sie arbeiten
- als Gesellen

g
- fünfeinhalb Wochen
- ich war
- in Südengland
- mit meinem Mann

h
- fahren
- mit unseren Kindern
- nach Deutschland
- wir werden
- nächstes Jahr

2   Was sind sie?

Three-word answers, please, e.g. **Er ist Schuhmacher.**

a   Anton lernt in Mittenwald Geigenbauen.
    Ist er Lehrling, Musiker, Bauer oder Ordensbruder? _____

b   Heinz Plöbst arbeitet im Café Mozart.
    Ist er Bäckermeister, Oberkellner, Glasbläser oder ist er der Chef? _____

c   Ich sitze auf dem Marktplatz und male Porträts.
    Bin ich Kunstschmied, Marktfrau, Bildhauer oder Straßenzeichner? _____

d   Adeline Schebesch hat eine Rolle bei *Jedermann*.
    Ist sie Opernsängerin, Sekretärin, Schauspielerin oder Verkäuferin? _____

e Frau Doktor Ketterer hat ein Sanatorium in Bad Mergentheim.
Ist sie Hausfrau, Frauenarzt, Ärztin oder Arzthelferin? _____

f Im Winter unterrichtet Franz Ruhm an der Skischule.
Ist er Schüler, Sportlehrer, Schuldirektor oder Landwirt? _____

g Horst Meier arbeitet an der Restaurierung des Regensburger Doms.
Ist er Archäologe, Metzger, Steinmetz oder Kirchendiener? _____

h Herr Triebe leitet die Dombauhütte in Regensburg.
Ist er Braumeister, Kellermeister, Bürgermeister oder Dombaumeister? _____

i Sieglind Bruhn spielt sehr gut Klavier.
Ist sie Puppenspielerin, Konzertpianistin, Straßenmusikantin oder Cellistin? _____

3   **Können müssen dürfen sollen wollen mögen**

The following sentences all need one of the above verbs; they are all used twice.
How do you say:

a I have to sing and dance. _____

b Would you like to visit the festival? _____

c Do the people of Salzburg like tourists? _____

d The women aren't allowed to wear costumes. _____

e Should one drink it or rub it in? _____

f A woman may not say no. _____

g You (**man**) can buy *Mozartkugeln* in the Getreidegasse. _____

h Roswitha Holz wants to remain in Salzburg. _____

i My husband had to go on a diet. _____

j Roland Techet can play the piano very well. _____

k Sebastian ought to go to bed, but he doesn't want to. _____

4   Supply the simple past of the verbs in brackets:

Wolfgang Amadeus Mozart (sein) _____ gebürtiger Salzburger. Schon als
Kind (können) _____ er sehr gut Klavier spielen. Mit sechs Jahren
(spielen) _____ er und seine Schwester Nannerl an den großen Höfen
Europas. Bis zu seinem 17. Lebensjahr (leben) _____ die Familie in
Salzburg, in der Getreidegasse Nummer neun. Im Jahre 1773 aber (ziehen)
_____ die Mozarts in ein anderes Haus in Salzburg. Für Wolfgang
(werden) _____ Salzburg aber bald zu klein. Mit 25 Jahren (gehen)
_____ er nach Wien. Dort (heiraten) _____ er Constanze Weber.
Er (sterben) _____ im Jahre 1791.

5   Each of these sentences needs the same verb to complete it, but used in a different
way each time. Write each one out in full, using the tense indicated on the left.

i

future	Die Ungers (essen) heute abend im Ratskeller
with **wollen**	Herr Unger (essen) einen Zwiebelrostbraten mit einem Semmelknödel
present	Frau Unger (essen) den Pfandlrostbraten
perfect	Gestern (essen) die Ungers Salzburger Nockerln
passive – present	Salzburger Nockerln (essen) in Salzburg gern

ii	future	Hermann Pfeil (herstellen) heute Pralinen
	with **müssen**	Er ist Pralinenmacher. Er (herstellen) Pralinen
	present	Er (herstellen) jeden Tag 40 verschiedene Sorten
	passive – present	Die Pralinen (herstellen) aus den edelsten Rohstoffen
	perfect	Gestern (herstellen) er hauptsächlich Barbara-Küsse
	passive – past	Diese Pralinen hier (herstellen) von Herrn Pfeil

6　The local know-alls are holding forth and as usual could not be more wrong! Make sure you put them right, incorporating the words in brackets:

EXAMPLE **Dieser Wein ist nicht so teuer wie der Sommeracher Rosenberg.**　(viel)
Ach was! Er ist *viel teurer*.

a Die Spätlese ist nicht so süß wie der Kabinett.

　　Doch, sie _____ .　(etwas)

b Jan Ole ist nicht so alt wie Sebastian.

　　Das stimmt nicht. Er _____ .　(4 Jahre)

c Der Tiger ist das schnellste Tier der Welt.

　　Quatsch! Der Gepard läuft _____ .　(viel)

d Der Ostfriesentee schmeckt gut ohne Kandis.

　　Ja, aber er _____ .　(mit)

e Trudi trägt den kürzesten Rock.

　　Das glaube ich nicht. Tinas Rock _____ !　(noch)

f Regensburg hat genau so viele alte Häuser wie Bamberg.

　　Nein, nein, Bamberg hat _____ .　(viel)

g Dieser Kirchturm ist der höchste in ganz Deutschland.

　　Das stimmt nicht. Der Ulmer Dom ist _____ .　(etwas)

　　Er hat den höchsten Kirchturm der Welt!

7　How would you say:

a have a nice stay! _____　　*g* excuse me! _____

b pleased to meet you _____　　*h* for example _____

c thank goodness! _____　　*i* Hello! (*in south Germany*) _____

d that's all _____　　*j* it all depends _____

e I'm sorry _____　　*k* may I? _____

f …and so on _____　　*l* have fun! _____

8　Transform these encyclopaedia entries into statements:

EXAMPLE **Wolfgang Amadeus Mozart ★ Salzburg 27.1.1756 ＋ Wien 5.2.1791**
Wolfgang Amadeus Mozart ist am siebenundzwanzigsten Januar 1756 in Salzburg geboren. Er ist am fünften Februar 1791 in Wien gestorben.

Martin Luther ★ Eisleben 10.11.1483　＋ Eisleben 18.2.1546
Johann Sebastian Bach ★ Eisenach 21.3.1685　＋ Leipzig 28.7.1750
Otto Fürst von Bismarck ★ Schönhausen 1.4.1815　＋ Friedrichsruh 30.7.1898

Can you cope?

You will find the key on page 95.

Verstehen Sie das? Which is the right answer?

1 Herr Pfeil tells you: **Wenn man bedenkt, daß alles nur von Hand hergestellt wird, und daß nur edelste Rohstoffe zur Verarbeitung gelangen, so könnte man wohl sagen, die Pralinen sind billig im Vergleich zur Industrieware.**

Does he mean
a the chocolates are cheap?
b they are expensive, but worth every pfennig?
c they are cheaper than those made in a factory?

2 When asked if he eats chocolates, Herr Pfeil replies: **Man kann ein stiller Genießer sein, auch für die Erzeugnisse, die man selber herstellen muß.**

Is he telling you
a he never likes things he's made himself?
b he isn't allowed to sample the products?
c it's quite possible to enjoy the things you've been making all day?

3 The press officer for Salzburg, Roswitha Holz, says: **Ich hoffe, daß mich das Schicksal nicht mehr von hier wegbringen wird.**

Do you think
a she hopes that fate will intervene to remove her from this spot?
b she would like to stay here for the rest of her life?
c she doesn't ever want to see the place again?

4 Helmut Ponstingl manages a restaurant in Salzburg. He says: **Salzburg hat etwas an sich, was man sehr schwer beschreiben kann.**

Is he saying
a Salzburg's a place that's difficult to describe?
b it's hard to find anything nice to say about Salzburg?
c there's something about the town that's hard to describe?

5 Franz Rahm the farming ski-instructor says: **Ich sehe das mit einem lachenden und mit einem weinenden Auge.**

Does he mean
a he's got something wrong with one of his eyes?
b he has a peculiar sense of humour?
c he can see both points of view?

6 A music student at the Mozarteum says: **Für neuere Musik ist das Echo hier sehr schlecht.**

Is he complaining that
a the concert hall has dreadful acoustics?
b there's scarcely any interest in modern music?
c you really need a room without an echo to hear new music properly?

7 A tourist tells Marcello: **Salzburg würde ich nicht als Urlaubsort empfehlen, es ist ein bißchen zu unruhig. Aber die Umgebung ist schön.**

Does she
a recommend Salzburg for a quiet holiday in beautiful surroundings?
b think Salzburg can be a noisy place to stay, but the area is nice?
c say Salzburg's a dreadful place, despite its beautiful surroundings?

8 Frau Unger talks about the Salzburg festival: **Man muß bis zum 15. Januar die Kartenwünsche einreichen und dann, wenn man Glück hat, bekommt man etwas.**

Is it true that
a you still need a slice of luck to get tickets even if you book early?
b you're certain to get tickets if you apply by 15 January?
c book early and you'll get some tickets, though perhaps not all you want?

9 The leader of the team which maintains Regensburg cathedral thinks: **Es ist für einen Steinmetzen eine wirklich große Aufgabe, ein solches Bauwerk für die Nachwelt erhalten zu können.**

Is he saying
a it's a worthwhile job preserving such a building for posterity?
b old buildings need a great deal of work to preserve them for posterity?
c Regensburg cathedral will keep stonemasons busy for generations?

10 Stimmt es oder stimmt es nicht? True or false?

Tick or cross the boxes:

a Fisch aus der Donau kann man gut essen. ☐

b Das Rezept für den Karmelitengeist ist kein Geheimnis. ☐

c Das 'Feuerwasser' soll man immer pur trinken. ☐

d Ein Steinmetz muß dreidimensional denken. ☐

e Im Land Salzburg hört man gar keine Volksmusik. ☐

f Eine Ausbildung von sieben Semestern dauert dreieinhalb Jahre. ☐

g Der Fasching findet am Anfang des Winters statt. ☐

h Im Frühling blüht alles wieder. ☐

i Jede Meistergeige ist ein einmaliges Instrument. ☐

j Die Stehplätze für die Festspiele sind nicht so teuer wie die Sitzplätze. ☐

k Normalsterbliche können immer billige Karten für die Festspiele bekommen. ☐

l Im Café Mozart spielen viele Stammgäste Schach. ☐

m Kuchen heißen in Österreich Mehlspeisen. ☐

n In einem typischen Wiener Café trinkt man schnell seinen Kaffee. ☐

o Der 'Salzburger Stier' ist kein Tier. ☐

p Ein Drachenflieger sieht die Landschaft wie aus den Augen eines Vogels. ☐

q Wolfgang Amadeus Mozart hat schon als Kind Konzerte gegeben. ☐

r In der Salzburger Musikschule 'Mozarteum' interessiert man sich nur für neue Musik. ☐

s Die vielen Touristen in Salzburg haben auch ihre Nachteile. ☐

t Die Stadt Salzburg soll eine der schönsten Städte der Erde sein. ☐

11 Was paßt nicht? There's an odd one out in all of these – except one!

a Which one wouldn't you see in Salzburg?
der Residenzplatz   der Staatliche Hofkeller   das Festspielhaus   die Festung

b Which of these couldn't you play?
der Kontrabaß   das Hackbrett   die Volksharfe   die Schreibstube

c Which one couldn't you eat?
der Fiaker   das Schlagobers   der Erdapfel   der Paradeiser

d Which of these could you see if you were hang-gliding?
die Alm   der See   das Tal   der Berg

e Which of these has a particular connection with Austria?
der Schnickschnack   das Schmalzgebäck   der Schilling   das Schellenrühren

f Which of these wouldn't you find among the concert-goers?
Normalsterbliche   Musiker   Schauspieler   Geschäftsschilder

g Which of these would you be most likely to see at the Salzburg Festival?
ein Fußballspiel   ein Mysterienspiel   ein Puppenspiel   ein Glockenspiel

h Which of these is an apt description of Salzburg in the tourist season?
unpersönlich   uninteressant   ungeheuer   unruhig

i Which of these couldn't you drink?
eine Melange   ein Veltliner   ein Gespritzter   ein Semmelknödel

j Which of these events has no particular connection with Salzburg?
das Adventsingen   das Erntedankfest   die Mozartwoche   die Osterfestspiele

k Which of these would you not use *Karmelitengeist* for?
zum Kochen   zum Desinfizieren   zum Trinken   zum Einreiben

Glossary

Anhalter – per Anhalter fahren   *to hitch-hike*
einfahren   *to drive in, enter, arrive*
einsteigen   *to board a vehicle*
die Fähre (-n)   *(cross-channel) ferry*
die Fremdsprache (-n)   *foreign language*
der Hamster (-)   *hamster*
die Himmelfahrt   *Ascension Day*
gestern   *yesterday*
die Großeltern (pl)   *grandparents*
der Maifeiertag   *May Day holiday*
die Maus (-̈e)   *mouse*
die Muttersprache (-n)   *native language*
Pfingsten   *Whitsuntide*
Russisch   *Russian language*
schicken   *to send*
der Stadtbummel (-)   *stroll through town*
der Tafelwein   *table wine*
wer?   *who?*
das Wort (-e)   *word*

Answers to exercises

Optional words are given in brackets. Alternative answers are given after (/).

Chapter 1

1i *a* die *b* Der *c* Die *d* der *e* Das

ii *a* eine *b* ein *c* ein *d* eine *e* ein

2 *a* Wo ist das Hotel Stern? *b* Wo ist der Dom? *c* Wo ist (hier) eine Bank? *d* Wo ist (hier) eine Drogerie? *e* Wo ist das Stadttheater? *f* Wo sind die Toiletten? *g* Wo ist die Rathausstraße? *h* Wo ist der Bahnhofsplatz? *i* Wo sind die Bremer Stadtmusikanten?

3 *a* Ich heiße Peter Fürst. Ich komme aus Heidelberg. Ich wohne in Bremen. Ich mache Urlaub in England. *b* Ich heiße Marianne Meyer. Ich komme aus Erfurt. Ich wohne in Berlin. Ich mache Urlaub in Duhnen. *c* Wir heißen Richter, Elfriede und Wilhelm Richter. Wir kommen aus Cuxhaven. Wir wohnen in Hamburg. Wir machen Urlaub in Heidelberg. *d* Wie heißen Sie? Woher kommen Sie? Wo wohnen Sie?

4 *a* sind *b* Sind *c* ist *d* ist *e* sind, ist *f* bin *g* sind

5i *a* Wo *b* Wie *c* Wo *d* Wie *e* Woher *f* Wie

ii *a* Wohnt sie im Strandhotel? *b* Ist Erfurt in der DDR? *c* Heißen Sie Joachim? *d* Ist das Sebastian? *e* Sind Sie/Sind sie hier auf Urlaub?

6i *a* Es *b* Sie *c* er *d* Er *e* Sie

ii *a* Er heißt Peter Fürst. Er kommt aus Heidelberg. Er wohnt in Bremen. Er macht Urlaub in England. *b* Sie heißt Marianne Meyer. Sie kommt aus Erfurt. Sie wohnt in Berlin. Sie macht Urlaub in Duhnen. *c* Sie heißen Richter, Elfriede und Wilhelm Richter. Sie kommen aus Cuxhaven. Sie wohnen in Hamburg. Sie machen Urlaub in Heidelberg.

7 *a* 7 *b* 8 *c* 70 *d* 13 *e* 43 *f* 34 *g* 2, 6 *h* 12 *i* 80

Chapter 2

1 *a* Haben *b* bist *c* bin *d* haben *e* hast *f* Sind *g* ist *h* habe, hat *i* ist

2i *a* einen Dom *b* ein Theater *c* einen Ratskeller *d* einen Park *e* ein Museum *f* eine Galerie

ii *a* eine *b* einen *c* einen *d* einen, eine *e* ein *f* einen *g* ein, einen, ein, eine *h* Haben Sie Briefmarken?

3 *a* keine *b* keine, keine *c* keinen, kein, keine, keine

4 die Kirchen, die Hotels, die Stadtpläne, die Märkte, die Städte, die Kioske, die Theater, die Postkarten, die Supermärkte, die Briefmarken, die Männer, die Gärten, die Apartmenthäuser, die Cafés, die Rathäuser

5i *a* Heide Debus wohnt jetzt in Lilienthal bei Bremen. Jetzt wohnt Heide Debus in Lilienthal bei Bremen. *b* Es gibt in Bremen viele Cafés. In Bremen gibt es viele Cafés. *c* Das Rathaus sehen Sie dort drüben. Sie sehen das Rathaus dort drüben.

ii *a* Wohnt Heide Debus jetzt in Lilienthal bei Bremen? *b* Gibt es in Bremen viele Cafés? *c* Sehen Sie das Rathaus dort drüben?

6 *a* schreibt *b* arbeitet *c* macht *d* kommen *e* wohnen *f* heißt *g* heiße *h* Arbeiten *i* heißt *j* Kommst *k* wohnt

7 *a* liegt *b* kauft *c* spielt *d* kaufen *e* gehe *f* finden *g* spielen *h* trinken

Chapter 3

1 *a* Was kosten die? *b* Was kostet die? *c* Was kostet der? *d* Was kostet das? *e* Was kostet die? *f* Was kostet das? *g* Was macht das? *h* Die Erdbeeren – was kosten die?

2 **Er heißt** Wolfgang Mönch und **er ist** 42 Jahre alt. **Er wohnt** in Beuel bei Bonn, aber **er arbeitet** in Köln. **Er hat** ein Auto, einen Ford. Im Moment **sitzt er** in einem Café und **schreibt** eine Postkarte nach England. **Sie sind** auf Urlaub hier in Bremen. Heute **machen sie** eine Hafenrundfahrt, dann **trinken sie** im Hotel Columbus eine Tasse Kaffee. Heute abend **essen sie** im Ratskeller, dann **gehen sie** ins Theater.

3 *a* Geben *b* fährst *c* esse *d* Gibt
e fährt *f* fahren *g* Ißt *h* fährt *i* ißt
j fahren

4 In Köln kann man ins Theater gehen. Man
kann einen Ausflug in das Siebengebirge
machen. Man kann den Dom und das
Rathaus besichtigen. Man kann am Rhein
spazierengehen. Man kann in den
Kaufhäusern gut einkaufen. Man kann eine
Dampferfahrt auf dem Rhein machen. Man
kann ein Fußballspiel im Müngersdorfer
Stadion ansehen.

5 *a* Was kann man hier machen? *b* Wo
kann man (hier) parken? *c* Wo kann man
(hier) gut essen? *d* Wo kann man (hier)
spazierengehen? *e* Wo kann man (hier)
gut einkaufen? *f* Was kann man im
Theater sehen? *g* Kann man das Rathaus
besichtigen? *h* Kann man eine
Dampferfahrt machen?

6 *a* Geben Sie *b* Kommen Sie *c* Besuchen
Sie *d* Sagen Sie *e* Bringen Sie *f* Fahren
Sie *g* Machen Sie

7i *a* Wie *b* Woher *c* Wie *d* Wie alt
e Wie *f* Wo *g* Was *h* Wo *i* Was für
ein *j* Wie *k* Was *l* Was für eine

ii *a* Wie alt ist er? *b* Wo wohnt er? *c* Wo
arbeitet er? *d* Woher kommt er? *e* Hat
er ein Auto? *f* Was für ein Auto hat er?

Chapter 4

1i *a* nehme, Nehmen *b* nimmst *c* nimmt
d Nehmen *e* nehmen

ii *a* Siehst *b* sieht *c* Sehen *d* sehe
e sehen

2 *a* möchte *b* Möchten *c* möchte
d möchtest *e* möchte *f* möchten

3 *a* einen, ein, die, einen, einen *b* keine,
keinen, ein *c* ein, Ein, Das, die

4 *a* mein . . . Er . . . *b* meine . . . Sie . . .
c meine . . . Sie . . . *d* meine . . . Sie . . .
e meinen . . . Er . . . *f* mein . . . Es . . .
g mein . . . Es . . . Mein . . .

5 *a* Seine . . . *b* Ihre . . . *c* Ihre . . . ihre . . .
d Ihre . . . *e* ihre . . . *f* Sein . . . *g* Ihr . . .
h Seine . . .

6 Wolfgang möchte eine Flasche Bier.
Susanne möchte ein Glas Orangensaft. Uwe
und Elke möchten zwei Kännchen Kaffee
und ein Stück Himbeertorte. Heide möchte
ein Stück Schwarzwälder (Kirschtorte) und
eine Tasse Kaffee. Sebastian möchte zwei
Stück Marzipankuchen mit Sahne und ein
Glas Milch. Catherin möchte ein Glas Tee
mit Zitrone. Karsten möchte ein Stück
Käsekuchen.

7 *a* Woher kommen Sie? *b* Wohnen Sie in
Bonn? *c* Wo wohnen Sie hier in Bonn?
d Haben Sie ein Haus oder eine Wohnung?
e Was für ein Auto haben Sie? *f* Sind Sie
verheiratet? *g* Wie lange sind Sie (schon)
verheiratet? *h* Wie heißt Ihre Frau? *i* Was
ist sie von Beruf? *j* Haben Sie Kinder?
k Gehen sie schon zur Schule? *l* Wie alt
sind sie? *m* Wie heißen sie? *n* Was kann
man in Bonn machen?

8 die Marken   die Mark   die Fahrpläne
die Schlüssel   die Töchter   die Radios
die Nächte   die Tassen   die Briefe
die Pfirsiche   die Gymnasien
die Fahrräder   die Kellnerinnen
die Haustiere   die Zimmer
die Kinder   die Sekretärinnen
die Gasthöfe

Chapter 5

1 *a* Nein, eine kleine. *b* Nein, die sauren.
c Nein, einen weißen. *d* Nein, lieber
einen süßen. *e* Nein, das große. *f* Nein,
den braunen.

2 *a* sauren *b* schwarz *c* grün *d* gelben,
roten *e* süß, sauer *f* Sommeracher
g lecker *h* kräftigen *i* alte, klein
j trockenen badischen

3 *a* Gut, ich nehme die. *b* Den nehme ich,
bitte. *c* Das nehme ich. *d* Das nehmen
wir. *e* Nein, wir nehmen die hier.
f Dann nehme ich den.

4 *a* Ich esse lieber Fleisch als Fisch. Ich
arbeite lieber in Deutschland als in England.
Ich wohne lieber in Bremen als in Greetsiel.
Ich spiele lieber Tennis als Fußball.
b Trinken Sie gern Orangensaft? Essen Sie
gern Käse? Arbeiten Sie lieber in einer
Schule? Essen Sie lieber ein Rührei?
c Ich esse am liebsten Schwarzwälder
(Kirschtorte). Ich trinke am liebsten Kaffee
mit Zucker und Sahne. Ich wohne am
liebsten in einem Hotel. Ich spiele am
liebsten Schach.

5 *a* vier Stunden *b* siebzehn Jahre *c* Jeden
Morgen *d* neunhundert Jahre *e* jede
Woche *f* acht Tage *g* Zehn Minuten

6 *a* Das ist *b* das sind *c* das sind *d* Das
sind *e* Es kann *f* es können

7 *a* neunzehn (19) *b* fünfundsiebzig (75),
siebenundfünfzig (57) *c* dreißig (30)
d sechsundachtzig (86) *e* neunzig Pfennig
(90 Pf.) *f* acht Mark zehn (8,10 DM)
g sechsundsiebzig Mark (76, – DM)

8 *a* Weinbrand *b* Sahne *c* Rotwein
d Äpfel *e* (is entirely correct) *f* Zitronen
g Schokolade *h* Pfirsiche

Chapter 6

1 *a* Ihrem *b* der *c* dem *d* der *e* meiner *f* einem *g* einer *h* ihren, Kindern

2 *a* Wie komme ich nach Leer? *b* Wie komme ich zur Wernigeroder Straße? *c* Wie komme ich zum Marktplatz? *d* Wie komme ich zur Weserbrücke? *e* Wie komme ich zu den Bremer Stadtmusikanten? *f* Wie komme ich nach Lilienthal? *g* Wie komme ich zur Insel Neuwerk?

3 *a* In einem *b* neben der *c* hinter dem *d* an der *e* vor dem *f* in dem *g* auf dem

4 *a* Ihrem *b* dein, deine *c* ihren *d* unserer *e* Mein *f* meine *g* sein *h* Ihrem

5 *a* nachmittags *b* mittwochs, freitags *c* morgens *d* Sonntags *e* nachts *f* Mittags *g* morgens, nachmittags

6 *a* Woher *b* Wohin *c* Wo *d* Wo *e* Woher *f* Wo *g* Wohin *h* Wo

7 *a* wissen *b* Weißt *c* weiß *d* Wissen *e* weiß *f* hältst *g* hält *h* Was halte *i* Was halten *j* Was halten

8 *a* Ich fahre mit dem (Fahr)rad zum Park. *b* Ich fahre mit dem Bus nach Greetsiel. *c* Ich fahre mit der Straßenbahn zum Einkaufszentrum. *d* Ich gehe zu Fuß zum Parkplatz. *e* Ich fahre mit dem Zug nach Berlin. *f* Ich fahre mit der Fähre nach Dover. *g* Ich fahre mit der Linie 4 zum Bahnhof. *h* Ich fahre mit dem Auto zum Anleger. *i* Ich fahre mit dem Dampfer nach Bremerhaven.

Chapter 7

1 *a* Der nächste Zug **fährt** um dreizehn Uhr **ab**. *b* Wann **kommt** der Zug in Frankfurt **an**? *c* Die Marktfrauen **stehen** um vier Uhr **auf**. *d* Um wieviel Uhr **fangen** wir mit der Arbeit **an**? *e* **Steigen** Sie am Marktplatz **aus**? *f* Marions Mittagspause **reicht** nie **aus**. *g* **Kommen** Sie **mit**? *h* Du **kommst** aus dem Bahnhof **heraus**, dann gehst du nach links. *i* **Kommen** Sie bitte **herein**!

2 aufstehen, mitkommen, aussteigen, einfahren, einsteigen, umsteigen, aussteigen, anfangen, abfahren, ankommen, herauskommen.

3 *a* Wann kommt der Bus (in Bonn) an? *b* Wo steigen Sie aus? *c* Wann stehen Sie auf? *d* Wann fangen Sie an? *e* Wann kann Herr Mönch vorbeikommen? *f* Wann müssen Sie aufstehen? *g* Wann kann ich anfangen?

4 *a* um, um *b* um *c* um *d* bis *e* um *f* von, bis *g* bis *h* um

5 *a* Was *b* Wann *c* Wie alt *d* Wie viele *e* Wo *f* Wie *g* Wann *h* Was für *i* Woher *j* Wie lange *k* Wieviel *l* Wohin *m* Wann *n* Wieviel

6i *a* Am Donnerstag und am Freitag bin ich in Würzburg. *b* Am Mittwoch kaufe ich die Fahrkarten. *c* Am Montag und am Sonntag spiele ich Tennis. *d* Am Wochenende mache ich Gartenarbeit./Am Samstag und am Sonntag mache ich Gartenarbeit. *e* Am Donnerstag stehe ich früh auf.

ii *a* an Wochentagen *b* an Wochenenden *c* an Dienstagen *d* an Feiertagen *e* an Ruhetagen *f* an Freitagen

7 *a* Nein, ich fange morgens um halb neun an. / . . . um acht Uhr dreißig an. *b* Die Fähre aus Harwich kommt um zwei Uhr nachmittags an. / . . . um vierzehn Uhr an. *c* Der Bus nach Oberneuland fährt um zehn Uhr fünf ab. / . . . um fünf (Minuten) nach zehn ab. *d* Der neue Kellner kann am Mittwoch anfangen. *e* Nein, Sie müssen in Neu-Ulm umsteigen.

8 *a* lang *b* einfache *c* wunderschöne *d* windreichen *e* frisch *f* weichgekochtes

Chapter 8

1 *a* hübsche *b* modernen, frisches *c* große *d* Schwarzer *e* frische *f* Wechselhaftes *g* Windreiche *h* verschiedene

2i *a* Ich komme aus der Schweiz. *b* Ich komme aus Spanien. *c* Ich komme aus der Sowjetunion. *d* Ich komme aus Frankreich. *e* Ich komme aus Schottland. *f* Wir kommen aus den USA. *g* Ich komme aus Griechenland. *h* (And finally: only you can answer this one!)

ii *a* nach *b* nach *c* in die *d* in die *e* nach

3 *a* Französisch *b* Deutsch *c* Latein, Griechisch *d* französische *e* auf deutsch *f* italienische *g* Russisch *h* Spanisch *i* deutscher

4 Pierre möchte in Bremen Kohl und Pinkel essen. Bernd möchte in Moskau den Kreml besichtigen/besuchen. Barbara möchte in den USA Disneyland besichtigen/besuchen. Wolfgang und Elke möchten in Österreich Winterurlaub machen. Paul möchte in Greetsiel ostfriesischen Tee trinken. Mein Mann und ich möchten in Hamburg im Hotel Vier Jahreszeiten übernachten. Jan Ole möchte in England seinen Brieffreund in Epping besuchen. Marion möchte in Südspanien ins Innere fahren. Richard möchte in Regensburg Geld verdienen.

5 *a* Richard will Lehrer werden. *b* Angelika möchte in der Industrie arbeiten. *c* Heide möchte nach Basel fahren. *d* Martin muß in Mailand umsteigen. *e* Man kann in der Sögestraße gut einkaufen. *f* Herr Haberland muß um halb sechs aufstehen/ . . . um 5.30 Uhr aufstehen. *g* Sie können von sechs (Uhr) bis neun Uhr frühstücken. *h* Sie kann eine Stunde bleiben.

6 *a* Bärbel hat im Januar Geburtstag. *b* Christoph und Michael haben im Februar Geburtstag. *c* Dorle hat im Oktober Geburtstag. *d* Harald und Trudi haben im Dezember Geburtstag. *e* Papa hat im Mai Geburtstag. *f* Herr Greiner und ich haben im März Geburtstag.

7 *a* Ich glaube, daß Trudi Lehrerin wird. *b* Ich glaube, daß ich bis Dienstag bleibe. *c* Ich glaube, daß wir nach Schottland fahren. *d* Ich glaube, daß Angelika eine Arbeitsstelle in Würzburg findet. *e* Ich glaube, daß *Deutsch direkt!* ausgezeichnet ist.

8 Es ist frustrierend, **ein Zimmer in der Stadtmitte zu suchen**. Es ist teuer, **in München zu wohnen**, aber es ist leicht, **Geld zu verdienen**. Es ist unmöglich, **jeden Tag zu arbeiten**. Es ist besser, **an Wochenenden oder in den Semesterferien zu arbeiten**. Es ist interessant, **Deutsch und Geschichte zu studieren**, aber es ist nicht leicht, **eine Arbeitsstelle in der Industrie zu finden.**

Chapter 9

1 *a* Pro Tag darf Christina tausend Kalorien essen. *b* Nein, Gift darf man nicht trinken. *c* Ja, ich darf ein Glas Weißwein trinken. *d* Nein, hier dürfen Sie nicht parken. *e* Er darf einmal in der Woche Kuchen essen. *f* Sie dürfen bis 21 Uhr aufbleiben. *g* Zum Frühstück darf ich ein Ei essen.

2 *a* Im Mai muß ich nach Wien fahren. *b* Ich muß zweimal am Tag Gymnastik machen. *c* Ja, leider müssen Sie eine Diät machen. *d* Sie muß 300 Kubikzentimeter Wasser trinken. *e* Er muß bis Ende Mai in Italien arbeiten. *f* Ja, mit dem Arzt müssen Sie einen Termin ausmachen. *g* Heute muß ich Brot, Obst und Milch kaufen. *h* Sie müssen um halb fünf aufstehen. / . . . um 4.30 Uhr . . .

3 *a* Hier kann man im Ratskeller gut essen. *b* Oh ja, ich kann sehr gut singen. *c* In Bad Mergentheim kann man eine Trinkkur machen. *d* Nein, in der Mittagspause kann ich nicht vorbeikommen. *e* Nein, in Regensburg kann Richard keine Arbeitsstelle finden. *f* Sie können morgen vormittag um 10 Uhr kommen. *g* Selbstverständlich kann ich Fahrrad fahren. *h* Dieses Jahr können wir im März oder im Mai Urlaub machen.

4 *a* muß *b* darf *c* darf *d* Können *e* Kann *f* muß *g* darf *h* muß *i* dürfen *j* müssen *k* Darf

5 *a* des Dorf(e)s *b* dieser Kirche *c* der Residenz *d* meiner Patienten *e* der Innenstadt *f* des Arztes

6 *a* Geben Sie *b* Komm, sag *c* Fahr *d* Trink *e* Kommt *f* Fahren Sie

7 *a* heute nachmittag *b* morgen *c* Montag vormittag *d* Heute abend *e* vormittags nachmittags *f* morgen vormittag *g* vormittags *h* Mittwoch nachmittags *i* abends *j* Sonntags

Chapter 10

1 *a* die *b* unsere *c* eine *d* den *e* die *f* die *g* die *h* meinen *i* das

2 *a* die *b* einer *c* dem *d* der *e* den *f* der *g* den *h* dem *i* den *j* an dem/am *k* dem *l* der

3 *a* flacher *b* süßer *c* jünger *d* flachere *e* billiger *f* älter *g* schöner *h* teurer *i* besseren

4 *a* älteste *b* am billigsten *c* modernste *d* beste, billigste *e* größte *f* schwersten *g* am lustigsten

5 *a* den *b* die *c* der *d* die *e* die *f* die *g* das *h* die *i* die

6 *a* Wann **finden** die Stadtführungen **statt**? *b* Marion **bleibt** abends bis halb zwölf **auf**. *c* Ein Ausflug nach Walhalla **dauert** zwei Stunden. *d* Herr Unger **verkauft** Lebensmittel in seinen Geschäften. *e* Richard Kerler **wird** bald Lehrer. *f* Bei Rot darf der Autofahrer nicht **weiterfahren**. *g* Um wieviel Uhr **stehst** du morgens **auf**? *h* Petra **trifft** Marion im Café Lindau. *i* Die Residenz zu Würzburg **gehört** dem Land Bayern *j* Der nächste Zug nach Berlin **fährt** um dreizehn Uhr **ab**. *k* Sie müssen eine Tablette mit etwas Wasser **einnehmen**. *l* Marions Mittagspause **reicht** nie **aus**, aber sie muß die Zeit nicht **nachholen**. *m* Christina **hält** ihre Diät **durch**, denn sie **nimmt** schnell **ab**.

7 In Würzburg kann man die Residenz und die Festung besichtigen. Man kann Frankenwein trinken. Man kann eine Weinprobe machen. Man kann ins Theater oder ins Kino gehen. Man kann im Residenzgarten oder am Main spazierengehen.

8 *a* Wo ist die Bushaltestelle? *b* Wie komme ich nach Spetzerfehn? *c* Wie komme ich am besten nach Würzburg? *d* Wo sind die Kaufhäuser? *e* Wohin fährt der Bus? *f* Wo gibt es hier in der Nähe eine Apotheke? *g* upstairs *h* home *i* into town *j* to Switzerland *k* straight ahead *l* left, round the corner

Chapter 11

1 *a* diese *b* dieses *c* diese *d* dieser
e dieses *f* Diese *g* dieser *h* diesem

2i *a* Welchen Wein nehmen Sie? *b* Welche
Klasse besuchst du? *c* Welches Brot
schmeckt am besten? *d* Welcher Wein ist
billiger? *e* Welche Patienten dürfen
Kuchen essen?

ii *f* Von welchem Gleis? *g* In welchem
Monat haben Sie Geburtstag? *h* An
welchem Tag schließen Sie? *i* Für welche
Führung möchten Sie Karten? *j* In
welcher Stadt arbeitet sie?

3 *a* einen Apfel *b* seinem Bruder *c* meine
Frau *d* der Kellnerin *e* seinen Kunden
f dem Hund *g* meiner Mutter eine
Postkarte *h* deinem Vater den Zucker

4 *a* ich, Sie *b* Sie *c* ich, mir *d* Sie
e ihn *f* mich *g* du mir *h* dir/Ihnen/
euch *i* uns

5 *a* Nein, die da! *b* Den da! *c* Nein, das
da! *d* Die da! *e* Den da!

6 *a* deiner *b* ihre *c* Ihre *d* seinen
e unserer *f* mein *g* meinen *h* Ihren
i ihre

7 *a* möchten *b* magst *c* mag *d* möchten
e mag *f* möchte *g* Mögen *h* möchte

8 *a* lieber als *b* schneller als *c* gern wie
d viel wie *e* teurer als *f* besser als
g süß wie *h* billiger als

Chapter 12

1 *a* Er gehört meiner Schwester. . *b* Diese
Mäuse gehören meinem Bruder. *c* Die
kleine Katze gehört meiner Mutter. *d* Die
Goldfische gehören mir. *e* Er gehört der
ganzen Familie.

2 *a* Gefällt es Ihnen *b* Du magst *c* gefällt
d arbeitet gern *e* gefallen *f* gefallen
g gefällt *h* mögen wir *i* mag

3 *a* Sebastian muß um Viertel nach acht ins
Bett. *b* Heide möchte heute nachmittag
nach München fahren. *c* Frau Bender
singt ungefähr dreimal in der Woche im
Stadttheater. *d* Herr Langwisch arbeitet
seit 17 Jahren bei Bünting in Leer. *e* Ich
fahre jetzt nach Hause. *f* Herr Haberland
ist seit 22 Jahren Gärtner im
Residenzgarten. *g* Ein paar Gäste bleiben
bis Weihnachten im Hotel. *h* Michael hat
morgen vormittag einen Termin bei Herrn
Doktor Bergis.

4 *a* wann *b* Wenn *c* wann *d* wenn
e Wann *f* Wenn *g* wann

5 *a* Nehmen Sie die Linie eins, wenn Sie aus
dem Bahnhof kommen. *b* Wir sind in fünf
Minuten in der Stadt, wenn wir mit der
Straßenbahn fahren. *c* Es ist nicht schwer,
eine Diät durchzuhalten, wenn man einen
Erfolg sieht. *d* Ich darf Alkohol trinken,
wenn ich etwas zum Essen weglasse.
e Meine Arbeit ist frustrierend, wenn ich
einem Jugendlichen nicht helfen kann.
f In Regensburg sind alle Hotels besetzt,
wenn große Kongresse dort stattfinden.

6 *a* Wenn Sie aus dem Bahnhof kommen,
nehmen Sie die Linie eins. *b* Wenn wir
mit der Straßenbahn fahren, sind wir in
fünf Minuten in der Stadt. *c* Wenn man
einen Erfolg sieht, ist es nicht schwer, eine
Diät durchzuhalten. *d* Wenn ich etwas
zum Essen weglasse, darf ich Alkohol
trinken. *e* Wenn ich einem Jugendlichen
nicht helfen kann, ist meine Arbeit
frustrierend. *f* Wenn große Kongresse
dort stattfinden, sind in Regensburg alle
Hotels besetzt.

7 *a* Der Maifeiertag ist am ersten Mai. *b* In
England ist der Maifeiertag am siebten Mai.
c Himmelfahrt ist am vierundzwanzigsten
Mai. *d* Der letzte Montag im Mai ist der
achtundzwanzigste. *e* Pfingstsonntag ist
der dritte Juni. *f* Der dritte Sonntag im
Juni ist der siebzehnte.

8 Irgendwann Irgendwie irgendwo
irgend jemand Irgendwas! irgendwohin!

Chapter 13

1 Wie heißt du? Nun, Tobias, kommst du aus
Bamberg? Du auch, Tina? Nein? Woher
kommst du? Aus München, so. Es gefällt dir
hier in Bamberg, oder? Schön! Gefällt es
euch allen hier in Bamberg? Aber
selbstverständlich, Bamberg ist ja eine
schöne Stadt.
Na ja, was für Hobbys habt ihr? Du Tina, du
spielst Geige, und du Tobias, du
interessierst dich für Sport. Habt ihr
Haustiere? Was! Drei Katzen! Süß! Nun,
Sonntag ist Erntedankfest. Geht ihr in die
Kirche? Was machst du in der Kirche, Tina?
Ah, du mußt was vorlesen. Du auch,
Tobias? Ihr singt ja wahrscheinlich auch.
Müßt ihr auch Obst aus dem Garten
mitbringen? Die Kirche sieht bestimmt
schön aus! Ich freue mich schon darauf.

2 *a* interessiert sich *b* befindet sich
c freuen uns *d* bedanke mich
e interessieren sich *f* mich umdrehe
g versteht euch *h* bemühe mich

3 *a* war *b* Warst *c* hatten *d* war
e waren *f* hatte *g* Waren *h* waren
i hatten

4 *a* Sie haben in einem kleinen Hotel gewohnt. *b* Sie haben Ostfriesentee getrunken. *c* Wir haben die Symphonie Nr 3 von Ludwig van Beethoven gehört. *d* Sie hat im Garten gearbeitet. *e* Ich habe eine Wanderung gemacht. *f* Gestern abend hat Joachim eine halbe Folge von *Dallas* gesehen.

5 Meine Eltern und ich haben um 8 Uhr gefrühstückt.   Tina hat Geige gespielt.   Tante Leni und Onkel Bernd haben Gartenarbeit gemacht.   Ich habe eine Horrorgeschichte gelesen.   Stefanie hat die Katze gefunden.

6 Papa ist um halb eins nach Hause gekommen.   Wir haben zu Mittag gegessen.   Onkel Bernd hat zu viel Wein getrunken.   Er ist ins Bett gegangen.   Er hat zwei Stunden geschlafen.   Mutti und Stefanie sind zum Supermarkt gefahren.   Tina und ich sind zu Hause geblieben.

7 *a* wirst *b* will *c* werden *d* wollen *e* werden *f* wollen . . . werden *g* Wird *h* willst . . . werden

8 Ja, ich lese gern, ich singe gern und ich höre gern Musik.   Mein Lieblingshobby ist Musik hören.   Am liebsten höre ich Operette, am allerliebsten die Operetten von Johann Strauß.   Nein, ich höre fast alle seine Operetten (sehr) gern.   Nein, Oper höre ich nicht so gern/weniger gern, ich höre viel lieber Musicals.

Chapter 14

1 *a* renoviert *b* gefallen *c* besichtigt *d* protestiert *e* erzählt *f* fotografiert *g* verkauft *h* entwickelt, vergrößert

2 *a* besucht *b* zugenommen *c* verloren *d* unternommen *e* spazierengegangen *f* übernachtet *g* zerstört *h* zurückgekommen *i* aufgewachsen

3 *a* Angelika möchte in Würzburg arbeiten, weil ihr Mann in Würzburg berufstätig ist. *b* Die Patienten trinken das Wasser, weil sie gesund werden wollen. *c* Der Tourist bleibt nicht sehr lange in Würzburg, weil er auf der Durchfahrt nach Kassel ist. *d* Wir sind gegen die neue Autobahn, weil sie den Wald zerstört. *e* Tina muß jeden Tag Geige üben, weil sie Musikerin werden will. *f* Richard Kerler führt Touristen durch Regensburg, weil er Geld verdienen muß. *g* Sebastian muß sofort ins Bett, weil er am nächsten Tag zur ersten Stunde Unterricht hat. *h* Frau Bender muß die jungen Mädchen spielen, weil sie eine leichte helle Stimme hat.

4 *a* In der Oberen Pfarre wird das Erntedankfest gefeiert. *b* Von Heidemarie Bender werden die jungen Mädchen gesungen. *c* Das Schloß wird seit etwa fünf Jahren renoviert. *d* Die deutsch-britische Gesellschaft wird von Joachim Kothe geleitet. *e* Alle Patienten werden medizinisch behandelt.

5 *a* Das Bier wird nach modernen Methoden gebraut. *b* Herrliches Brot wird aus dem Mehl gebacken. *c* Der Wald wird durch die neue Autobahn zerstört. *d* Eine Million Flaschen Wein werden von dem Staatlichen Hofkeller produziert. *e* Die Trauben werden von den Frauen geschnitten und von den Männern zum Wagen getragen.

6 *a* Die Kühe werden zweimal am Tag gemolken. *b* Nein, die schönen Häuser werden nicht zerstört. *c* Ja, viel Tee wird in Ostfriesland getrunken. *d* Das Volkacher Weinfest wird von Andrea Wägerle eröffnet. *e* Das Bier wird nach modernen Methoden produziert. *f* Der Gymnastikkurs für Seniorinnen wird von Ilse Wojaczek geleitet.

7 *a* sehen, genügen *b* bestellen *c* sein *d* aufstehen *e* gefallen *f* bringen *g* gewinnen *h* entwickeln *i* ausbauen, umbauen

8i *a* In der Nähe eines Flusses, dieses Waldes, der Geschäfte, der Kirche *b* am Rande dieser Stadt, des Marktplatzes, einer Siedlung, der Berge *c* im Herzen des Dorfes, Frankens.

ii *a* der Landschaft, der Landschaft *b* des Kindes, dem Kind *c* der Touristen, den Touristen *d* meines Hundes, meinem Hund

Chapter 15

1 *a* die Würzburger Residenz *b* die Bremer Stadtmusikanten *c* der Volkacher Ratsherr *d* die Bad Mergentheimer Trinkkur *e* das Jever Bier *f* der Regensburger Dom/ der Bamberger Dom *g* die Bamberger Symphoniker *h* der Dinkelsbühler Nachtwächter *i* die Berliner Philharmoniker

2 *a* wollten *b* sollte *c* durfte *d* konnten *e* hatte *f* mußte *g* wollte *h* mochte *i* mußten *j* wollte, mußte

3 *a* Die Windmühle **wurde** vor vielen Jahren von Theo Steenblock und seiner Familie **restauriert**. *b* Frau Wiemers Garten **wird** im Moment **angelegt**. *c* Das Volkacher Weinfest **wurde** 1983 von Andrea Wägerle **eröffnet**. *d* Zur Zeit **wird** jährlich sehr viel Frankenwein **exportiert**. *e* Nächste Woche **werden** rund 400 Weine aus ganz Franken **geprüft**. *f* Die schönen Brote, die Sie heute morgen in der Kirche gesehen haben, **wurden** von Herrn Hoh **gebacken**. *g* Die Wurstküche **wurde** im 12. Jahrhundert **gebaut**. *h* Die Schutzgemeinschaft Alt-Bamberg paßt auf, daß die schönen alten Häuser nicht **zerstört werden**.

4 *a* dagegen *b* Darunter *c* Darin *d* Dadurch *e* dagegen *f* davon *g* dafür *h* Darin *i* darauf

5 *a* dem *b* die *c* die *d* die *e* unserem *f* dem, der *g* dem *h* die *i* den *j* den *k* einem *l* dem nördlichsten

6 *a* Heide **befindet sich** in der Vorhalle des Bremer Hauptbahnhofes. *b* Der Ausgang **führt** in Richtung Bahnhofsvorplatz. *c* Bei der Bahnhofsauskunft **bekommt** man Informationen. *d* Wann **finden** die Führungen **statt**? *e* Eine Führung **dauert** normalerweise zwei Stunden. *f* Die Touristen **besichtigen** den Regensburger Dom. *g* Man **riecht** den Duft der historischen Wurstküche. *h* Das Schiff **gehört** der Familie Klinger. *i* Verkehrsprobleme **kommen** oft in älteren Städten **vor**. *j* Die Wurstküche **stellt** jedes Jahr kilometerweise Würstchen **her**.

7 *a* Ist Hilke jünger als Hajo? *b* Ist Nancy die jüngste? *c* Wer ist der älteste? *d* Arbeitet Hajo besser als Johnny? *e* Helfen die Kinder gern bei der Arbeit? *f* Wer hilft am liebsten bei der Arbeit?

8 Regensburg hat eine 2000-jährige Geschichte. Im Mittelalter war die Stadt ein politisches und kirchliches Zentrum. Im Alten Rathaus tagte 1663 das erste deutsche Parlament. Der Regensburger Dom ist eine der wichtigsten gotischen Kirchen in Deutschland. Interessant im Dom sind die vielen bunten Glasfenster aus dem Mittelalter. Die berühmte Steinerne Brücke ist fast 850 Jahre alt. Von der Brücke hat man einen schönen Blick über die Stadt mit der Silhouette der vielen Türme und Häuser. Riechen Sie den Duft der historischen Wurstküche? Die historische Wurstküche ist berühmt für selbstgemachte Würstchen und für das selbstgemachte Sauerkraut. Die Würstchen schmecken einfach herrlich! Heute nachmittag machen wir eine kurze Fahrt auf der romantischen blauen Donau.

Chapter 16

1 *a* Geschäftsführerin *b* Pfarrer *c* Berufsberaterin *d* Landwirt *e* Opernsängerin *f* Sekretärin *g* Ärzte *h* Pralinenmacher *i* Archäologe *j* Kunstschmied *k* Schülerinnen *l* Winzer *m* Studentin

2 *a* stand *b* wohnten *c* machte *d* verband *e* mußte, wollte *f* war, kaufte *g* gab *h* saßen *i* mußte, ausbrach

3 *a* wäre *b* hätte *c* würde *d* könnte *e* Würde *f* Möchtest *g* würde, hätte *h* Würden *i* könnte *j* wären, müßten

4 *a* die *b* der *c* den *d* die *e* denen *f* der *g* die *h* das *i* das *j* denen

5 Mittwoch vormittag **wollen** wir eine Stadtführung **machen**. Am Nachmittag **wollen** wir mit dem Schiff zur Walhalla fahren. Mittwoch abend **wollen** wir im Stadttheater die *Fledermaus* **sehen**. Donnerstag vormittag **wollen** wir im Karmelitenkloster Karmelitengeist **probieren**. Zu Mittag **wollen** wir in der historischen Wurstküche Würstchen mit Sauerkraut **essen**. Nach dem Mittagessen **wollen** wir das Alte Rathaus **besichtigen**. Am Abend **wollen** wir bei Herrn Unger eine Weinprobe **machen**. Am nächsten Morgen **wollen** wir zu Fuß zum Fischmarkt **gehen**. Dann **wollen** wir nach Hause **fahren**.

6 Mittwoch vormittag **haben** wir eine Stadtführung **gemacht**. Am Nachmittag **sind** wir mit dem Schiff zur Walhalla **gefahren**. Mittwoch abend **haben** wir im Stadttheater die *Fledermaus* **gesehen**. Donnerstag vormittag **haben** wir im Karmelitenkloster Karmelitengeist **probiert**. Zu Mittag **haben** wir in der historischen Wurstküche Würstchen mit Sauerkraut **gegessen**. Nach dem Mittagessen **haben** wir das Alte Rathaus **besichtigt**. Am Abend **haben** wir bei Herrn Unger eine Weinprobe **gemacht**. Am nächsten Morgen **sind** wir zu Fuß zum Fischmarkt **gegangen**. Dann **sind** wir nach Hause **gefahren**.

7 *a* Regensburg ist größer als Etterzhausen. *b* Februar ist kürzer als März. *c* Frau Peithner ist jünger als ihr Mann. *d* Der Sommer ist wärmer als der Winter. *e* Andreas Festkleid ist länger als ihre normalen Kleider. *f* Die Bahnhofsgaststätte ist teurer als das Bistro.

Chapter 17

1 *a* In diesem Haus werden neunzig Studenten wohnen. *b* Wir werden vor dem Parlament in Bremen protestieren. *c* Sie wird Englisch und Geschichte studieren. *d* Er wird heute abend die Bilder vergrößern. *e* Ich werde Mozarts Geburtshaus und die Festung besichtigen.

2 *a* Ich gehe auf den Markt, um Blumen und Gemüse zu kaufen. *b* Frau Wiemer fährt mittags nach Hause, um Joghurt und Obst zu essen. *c* Fünfzigtausend Gäste kommen jedes Jahr nach Bad Mergentheim, um eine Kur zu machen. *d* Wir brauchen acht bis zehn Wochen, um ein gutes Bier zu brauen. *e* Die Touristen kommen abends aus ihren Zimmern heraus, um einen kleinen Stadtbummel zu machen. *f* Katrin fährt nach Würzburg, um die Residenz und den Rosengarten zu besichtigen. *g* Die Steinhäusers sind nach Bamberg gegangen, um auf dem Marktplatz zu protestieren.

3 *a* An die tausend Quadratmeter. *b* Grob gerechnet etwa 5.000 Kilogramm. *c* Hundert Gramm. *d* Zirka 150.000 Fläschchen im Jahr. *e* Zehn Mark und zwanzig. *f* In der Nummer neun. *g* Ungefähr 4.000 Stück. *h* Etwa 15 Kilometer. *i* Eine halbe Stunde. *j* Sie ist 310 Meter lang. *k* Seit 16 Jahren. *l* 50 Pfennig das Stück. *m* Es hat ungefähr 150 Quadratmeter Wohnfläche. *n* OHZ-TE 66.

4 *a* Woher *b* Seit wann *c* Wie *d* Wieviele *e* Warum *f* Was *g* Wie lange *h* Wer *i* Wo *j* Welche *k* Wann

5 die Flüsse   die Bäume   die Blätter   die Domtürme   die Zentren   die Shantys   die Erzeugnisse   die Gymnasien   die Stockwerke   die Kaufleute   die Restaurants   die Sanatorien   die Hobbys   die Ordensbrüder   die Prüfungen   die Regensburgerinnen   die Chefs   die Bauten

6 *a* Der saure Regen kommt aus den Industriegebieten. *b* Einige Zutaten für den Karmelitengeist kommen aus dem Garten des Karmelitenklosters. *c* Die Fische, die die Hofmeisters verkaufen, kommen aus der Donau. *d* Die Touristen, die nach Rothenburg kommen, kommen aus der ganzen Welt. *e* Frau Schistowskis Diät kommt aus einer Zeitschrift.

7 *a* die älteste *b* das größte und schönste *c* Die meisten *d* die eleganteste *e* die besten *f* der schönsten *g* das kleinste *h* die wichtigste und härteste *i* die beliebteste

8 *a* mag *b* darf *c* müssen *d* will *e* soll *f* kann

Chapter 18

1 *a* einem kleinen Dorf in Ostfriesland *b* einen alten Campingbus *c* der jungen Weinkönigin von Volkach *d* dem herrlichen Würzburger Barockschloß *e* dem Herzstück der Salzburger Festspiele *f* einem englischen Mysterienspiel *g* dem Vater Mozarts *h* des berühmten Dirigenten *i* dem Mönchsberg und dem Kapuzinerberg

2i Sandy und seine Frau fahren am sechsundzwanzigsten Mai mit dem Auto in die Schweiz.   Tracy fährt am neunten Juni per Anhalter nach Spanien.   Onkel Peter und Tante Helen fahren am sechzehnten Juni mit dem Schiff in die USA.   Ich fahre am siebten Juli mit dem Bus nach Salzburg.   Meine Eltern fahren am einunddreißigsten Juli mit dem Zug in die Türkei.

ii *a* Am sechsundzwanzigsten Mai fahren Sandy und seine Frau mit dem Auto in die Schweiz. Am neunten Juni fährt Tracy per Anhalter nach Spanien. Am sechzehnten Juni fahren Onkel Peter und Tante Helen mit dem Schiff in die USA. Am siebten Juli fahre ich mit dem Bus nach Salzburg. Am einunddreißigsten Juli fahren meine Eltern mit dem Zug in die Türkei.

3 *a* Gesellen *b* Studenten *c* Kollege *d* Herrn *e* Jungen *f* Steinmetzen *g* Student *h* Herr *i* Gesellen ... Herrn *j* Steinmetz *k* Gesellen *l* Komponisten

4i *a* In Mittenwald treiben die Schellenrührer den Winter aus. *b* Die neue Autobahn unterbricht unseren Spaziergang. *c* Herr Maller wählt immer selbst das Holz aus. *d* Dorle und ihre Geschwister verstehen sich gut. *e* Die Universität Regensburg errichtet Studentenwohnungen in der Altstadt. *f* Die Studenten sitzen im Gemeinschaftsraum zusammen. *g* Wir interessieren uns nicht für neue Musik. *h* Die Grünen beschäftigen sich mit Umweltproblemen. *i* Ich freue mich auf das Erntedankfest. *j* Wir gehen sehr oft im Wald spazieren.

ii *e* Die Universität Regensburg hat Studentenwohnungen in der Altstadt errichtet. *i* Ich habe mich auf das Erntedankfest gefreut. *j* Wir sind sehr oft im Wald spazierengegangen.

iii *a* In Mittenwald wird der Winter von den Schellenrührern ausgetrieben. *b* Unser Spaziergang wird durch die neue Autobahn unterbrochen. *e* Studentenwohnungen werden von der Universität Regensburg in der Altstadt errichtet.

iv *b* Die neue Autobahn wird unseren Spaziergang unterbrechen. *f* Die Studenten werden im Gemeinschaftsraum zusammensitzen. *h* Die Grünen werden sich mit Umweltproblemen beschäftigen.

v *a* In Mittenwald wollen die Schellenrührer den Winter austreiben. *f* Die Studenten dürfen im Gemeinschaftsraum zusammensitzen. *j* Wir können sehr oft im Wald spazierengehen.

5 *a* Am Nachmittag schläft der Bäckermeister drei Stunden. *b* Wir wohnen seit 40 Jahren in Regensburg. *c* Die Premiere findet am 29. Juli um fünf Uhr statt./... um siebzehn Uhr statt. *d* Marcello könnte stundenlang sitzen und zugucken. *e* Die Stadtführungen finden zweimal am Tag statt. *f* Ruhetag hat die Wurstküche einmal im Jahr, zu Weihnachten. *g* Die Ausbildung eines Kunstschmiedes dauert elf Jahre. *h* Die Restaurierung des Regensburger Doms begann vor hundert Jahren. *i* Das Schellenrühren kann man am Unsinnigen Donnerstag sehen. *j* Die Sommerfestspiele dauern von Ende Juli bis Ende August.

6 *a* Wenn man es eilig hat, kann man im Bistro schnell Würstchen und Kartoffelsalat zu sich nehmen. *b* Wenn man über die Steinerne Brücke geht, hat man einen schönen Blick über die Stadt. *c* Wenn sie eine Vorstellung hat, muß Frau Bender eine Stunde vorher im Theater sein. *d* Wenn er zur ersten Stunde Unterricht hat, muß Sebastian früh ins Bett. *e* Wenn man Glück hat, bekommt man Karten für die Festspiele. *f* Wenn die Grünen einen kranken Baum finden, malen sie ein Kreuz darauf. *g* Wenn die Touristen in Regensburg ankommen, brauchen sie Hotelzimmer.

7 *a* der Schellen *b* eines jungen Mannes *c* des Schwarzwaldes *d* der alten Häuser *e* dieser evangelischen Kirche *f* Tinas *g* eines kleinen Flusses *h* des täglichen Lebens *i* der alten Seeleute *j* Europas *k* des Bremer Hauptbahnhofes *l* der Steinernen Brücke *m* Herbert von Karajans

Chapter 19

1 *a* In Jever gibt es eine Brauerei, wo das Bier nach ganz modernen Methoden gebraut wird. *b* Die Wurstküche ist ein altes Restaurant, wo man herrliche Würstchen mit hausgemachtem Senf essen kann. *c* Wir waren ein paar Tage in Würzburg, wo wir die Residenz und die Festung besichtigt haben. *d* Die Universität Regensburg baut Studentenwohnheime in der Altstadt, wo etwa 90 Studenten wohnen werden.

e Das Café Mozart ist ein typisches Wiener Café, wo man Zeitung lesen kann. *f* Bei Berthold Unger finden Weinproben statt, wo 30 bis 40 Sorten Wein probiert werden. *g* Zwanzig Kilometer von Salzburg liegt Oberndorf, wo 1816 *Stille Nacht* geschrieben wurde. *h* Die Steinhäusers und ihre Kinder sind nach Bamberg gegangen, wo sie gegen die neue Autobahn protestiert haben.

2 *a* Das Skilaufen, das Schwimmen, das Radfahren *b* das Drachenfliegen *c* Das Maskenschnitzen *d* Das Skispringen *e* das Biertrinken *f* das Klavierspielen

3 *a* Die Festspiele kann man nicht besuchen, weil es keine Karten für Normalsterbliche gibt. *b* Ich muß viel Wein trinken, aber ich trinke auch gerne viel Wein. *c* Ich versuche in die Festspiele zu gehen, wenn ich einen Stehplatz bekommen kann. *d* Die Schutzgemeinschaft Alt-Bamberg paßt auf, daß die wertvollen Häuser nicht zerstört werden. *e* Für jedes Wohnheim gibt es einen Gemeinschaftsraum, so daß die Studenten auch in einer Gruppe zusammensitzen können. *f* Es gibt im Residenzgarten genug Arbeit für zwölf Gärtner, denn dieser Garten ist sehr groß. *g* Das Wasser von der Quelle ist gesund, aber es schmeckt nicht gut. *h* Unsere Stammgäste bleiben länger sitzen, bis sie mit dem Schach fertig sind. *i* Es ist sehr schlimm, daß die Bäume sterben, denn wir brauchen den Wald zum Leben. *j* Es ist heute für Herrn Kroll ein besonderer Sieg, denn er ist zum letzten Mal gesprungen.

4 *a* von meinem *b* zum ersten *c* in dem/im *d* aus *e* Bei diesem schönen *f* für selbstgemachte *g* des Waldes wegen *h* bei Herrn *i* zu einer *j* bei der *k* auf *l* bei *m* zu *n* von *o* nach

5 *a* Wann wirst du zehn? *b* Wieviel/Wie viele Studenten werden hier wohnen? *c* Tina will Musikerin werden. *d* Wo wird *Jedermann* gespielt? *e* Die Skischule wurde von Riki Spieß gegründet. *f* Ich werde bald 76. *g* Zwölf Schüler werden ausgewählt. *h* Das werde ich morgen bestellen./Ich werde es morgen bestellen. *i* Für Mozart wurde Salzburg zu klein./Salzburg wurde für Mozart zu klein.

6 *a* In Jever braut man Bier aus Hopfen, Gerste und Wasser. *b* Silvia Kirsch macht Schmuck aus Glas. *c* Der Teufel und seine Großmutter sind Figuren aus Stein. *d* Andrea Wägerles Dirndlkleid ist aus Seide und Brokat. *e* Die Würstchen in der Wurstküche sind aus Schweinefleisch. *f* Eine Geige ist aus drei verschiede**n**en. Holzart**en**. *g* Die Pralinen werden aus den edelst**en** Rohstoff**en** hergestellt. *h* Aus dem Mehl wird herrliches Brot gebacken. *i* Herr Peithner ist Kunstschmied. Er stellt Kunstwerke aus Schmiedeeisen her.

7   Mittenwald ist eine kleine Stadt in Bayern. Dort ist der Geigenbau zu Hause. Qualitätsinstrumente werden in der weltbekannten Geigenbauschule gebaut. Eine Geige ist aus drei verschiedenen Holzarten. Auch aus Holz sind die Mittenwalder Holzmasken, die hobbymäßig von vielen Geigenbauern geschnitzt werden. Die traditionelle Holzmaske ist das Gesicht eines jungen Mannes. Man trägt diese Maske mit einem bunten Kostüm zum Fasching. Eine berühmte Faschingstradition in Mittenwald ist das (berühmte) Schellenrühren am Unsinnigen Donnerstag. Durch den Lärm der Schellen wollen die jungen Männer den kalten Winter vertreiben. Die Schellenrührer tragen eine kurze Lederhose, ein weißes Hemd und eine Holzmaske. Sie ziehen von Gaststätte zu Gaststätte und trinken dabei sehr viel Bier.

8   *a* Ich habe in Innsbruck Sport studiert. *b* In Bamberg sind viele Bäume gestorben. *c* Jan Ole hat Mathe und Englisch nicht so gern gehabt.   *d* Wir sind im Café Mozart in der Salzburger Getreidegasse gewesen. *e* Frau Schretzenmayr ist dieses Jahr in den Schwarzwald gefahren.   *f* Wie weit bist du gesprungen, Robert?   *g* Haben Sie das Kostüm anprobiert?   *h* Wieviele Wohnungen haben Sie in der Stadt gebaut? *i* Was haben Sie gemacht, um Geld zu verdienen?

Chapter 20

1   *a* Sie müssen eine Tablette eine Stunde vor dem Schlafengehen mit etwas Wasser einnehmen.   *b* Sepp Laugner kam nach dem Krieg zu Fuß nach Dinkelsbühl. *c* Meine neue Wohnung liegt etwa zehn Minuten mit dem Auto von der Innenstadt entfernt.   *d* Den Pfandlrostbraten hat Frau Unger gestern abend im Café Mozart bestellt.   *e* Ungefähr seit 1945 fährt meine Familie auf der Donau./ Auf der Donau fährt meine Familie ungefähr seit 1945. *f* Sie arbeiten drei Jahre als Gesellen bei einem Meister.   *g* Ich war fünfeinhalb Wochen mit meinem Mann in Südengland. *h* Wir werden nächstes Jahr mit unseren Kindern nach Deutschland fahren.

2   *a* Er ist Lehrling.   *b* Er ist Oberkellner. *c* Sie sind Straßenzeichner.   *d* Sie ist Schauspielerin.   *e* Sie ist Ärztin.   *f* Er ist Sportlehrer.   *g* Er ist Steinmetz.   *h* Er ist Dombaumeister.   *i* Sie ist Konzertpianistin.

3   *a* Ich muß singen und tanzen.   *b* Möchten Sie/Möchtest du/Möchtet ihr die Festspiele besuchen?   *c* Mögen die Salzburger die Touristen?   *d* Die Frauen dürfen keine Kostüme tragen.   *e* Soll man es trinken oder einreiben?   *f* Eine Frau darf nicht nein sagen.   *g* Man kann Mozartkugeln in der Getreidegasse kaufen.   *h* Roswitha Holz will in Salzburg bleiben.   *i* Mein Mann mußte eine Diät machen.   *j* Roland Techet kann sehr gut Klavier spielen. *k* Sebastian soll ins Bett gehen, aber er will nicht.

4   Wolfgang Amadeus Mozart war gebürtiger Salzburger. Schon als Kind konnte er sehr gut Klavier spielen. Mit sechs Jahren spielten er und seine Schwester Nannerl an den großen Höfen Europas. Bis zu seinem 17. Lebensjahr lebte die Familie in Salzburg, in der Getreidegasse Nummer neun. Im Jahre 1773 aber zogen die Mozarts in ein anderes Haus in Salzburg. Für Wolfgang wurde Salzburg aber bald zu klein. Mit 25 Jahren ging er nach Wien. Dort heiratete er Constanze Weber. Er starb im Jahre 1791.

5i   Die Ungers werden heute abend im Ratskeller essen. Herr Unger will einen Zwiebelrostbraten mit einem Semmelknödel essen. Frau Unger ißt den Pfandlrostbraten. Gestern haben die Ungers Salzburger Nockerln gegessen. Salzburger Nockerln werden in Salzburg gern gegessen.

ii   Hermann Pfeil wird heute Pralinen herstellen. Er ist Pralinenmacher. Er muß Pralinen herstellen. Er stellt jeden Tag 40 verschiedene Sorten her. Die Pralinen werden aus den edelsten Rohstoffen hergestellt. Gestern hat er hauptsächlich Barbara-Küsse hergestellt. Diese Pralinen hier wurden von Herrn Pfeil hergestellt.

6   *a* Doch, sie ist etwas süßer.   *b* Er ist 4 Jahre älter.   *c* Der Gepard läuft viel schneller.   *d* Ja, aber er schmeckt besser mit (Kandis).   *e* Tinas Rock ist noch kürzer!   *f* Nein, nein, Bamberg hat viel mehr.   *g* Der Ulmer Dom ist etwas höher.

7   *a* angenehmen Aufenthalt!   *b* (es) freut mich   *c* Gott sei Dank!   *d* das wär's *e* es tut mir leid   *f* und so weiter *g* Entschuldigung/Entschuldigen Sie *h* zum Beispiel   *i* grüß Gott!   *j* es kommt darauf an   *k* darf ich?   *l* viel Spaß!

8   Martin Luther ist am zehnten November 1483 in Eisleben geboren. Er ist am achtzehnten Februar 1546 in Eisleben gestorben.
Johann Sebastian Bach ist am einundzwanzigsten März 1685 in Eisenach geboren. Er ist am achtundzwanzigsten Juli 1750 in Leipzig gestorben.
Otto Fürst von Bismarck ist am ersten April 1815 in Schönhausen geboren. Er ist am dreißigsten Juli 1898 in Friedrichsruh gestorben.

Key to Can you cope?

1 *b* **2** *c* **3** *b* **4** *c* **5** *c* **6** *b* **7** *b* **8** *a* **9** *a*

10 *a* √ *b* × *c* × *d* √ *e* × *f* √ *g* × *h* √ *i* √
j √ *k* × *l* √ *m* √ *n* × *o* √ *p* √ *q* √ *r* ×
s √ *t* √

11 *a* der Staatliche Hofkeller *b* die
Schreibstube *c* der Fiaker *d* all of
them! *e* der Schilling *f* Geschäftsschilder
g ein Mysterienspiel *h* unruhig *i* ein
Semmelknödel *j* das Erntedankfest
k zum Kochen

Scoring system:

Give yourself one point for each correct
answer; possible maximum 40 points.

Anything over 34 is excellent – you clearly
know *Deutsch direkt!* inside out.

Scores above 25 are very good indeed –
perhaps look again at any section you know
caught you out.

If you didn't manage 25, look again at Chapters
16–20, on which all these questions were based.

List of exercises

Chapter 9

1 present tense of **dürfen**; word order
2 present tense of **müssen**; word order
3 present tense of **können**; word order
4 word order after a 'modal' verb
5 genitive case: 'of the'
6 commands: **du, ihr, Sie**
7 times: single occasions and repeated events

Chapter 10

1 prepositions always with the accusative
2 prepositions with both accusative and dative
3 adjectives – 'comparative' form
4 adjectives – 'superlative' form
5 relative pronouns
6 present tense of verbs
7 word order after a 'modal' verb
8 questions and directions

Chapter 11

1 **dieser**
2 **welcher**
3 direct and indirect object
4 personal pronouns
5 **den, die, das**: used demonstratively
6 possessives
7 **mögen: ich mag** and **ich möchte**
8 comparisons

Chapter 12

1 **gehören**
2 'liking': **gern, mögen** or **gefallen**?
3 word order: 'when' before 'where'
4 **wann, wenn**
5 word order after **wenn**: subordinate clauses
6 word order in main clauses: compound sentences
7 ordinal numbers; dates
8 **irgend-**

Chapter 13

1 **du** and **ihr**
2 present tense of 'reflexive' verbs
3 simple past of **sein** and **haben**
4 perfect tense with **haben**: word order
5 perfect tense: the past participle
6 perfect tense with **sein**
7 **werden** and **wollen**
8 comparisons with **gern, lieber, am liebsten** etc

Chapter 14

1 perfect tense: past participles of 'inseparable' verbs
2 perfect tense: past participles of 'separable' verbs
3 word order after **weil**: 'auxiliary' verbs in subordinate clauses
4 passive – present tense
5 passive and active verbs
6 passive and active verbs
7 infinitives
8 genitive case: 'of the', of proper names; **wegen** with genitive or dative

Chapter 15

1 names of towns as adjectives
2 simple past: 'modal' verbs and **haben**
3 passive: present and past tenses
4 **davor, daraus** etc
5 prepositions with both accusative and dative
6 present tense
7 questions using comparatives and superlatives
8 adjectives

Chapter 16

1 jobs: masculine and feminine forms
2 simple past of 'weak' and 'strong' verbs
3 'conditional' form
4 relative pronouns
5 **wollen**
6 perfect tense
7 comparisons

Chapter 17

1 future tense; word order
2 **um . . . zu** with infinitive
3 numbers
4 question words
5 plurals
6 origins: **kommen aus**
7 superlatives
8 'modal' verbs

Chapter 18

1 nouns in apposition
2 word order: 'when' and 'how' before 'where'
3 'weak' nouns
4 verbs: revision of tenses
5 expressions of time
6 **wenn** clauses; word order
7 genitive case

Chapter 19

1 word order in subordinate clauses
2 verbal nouns
3 word order in subordinate clauses and clauses of equal importance
4 prepositions
5 **werden**
6 what things are made of
7 adjectives
8 perfect tense

Chapter 20

1 word order
2 **Was sind sie?** = jobs
3 'modal' verbs
4 simple past
5 revision of tenses
6 comparatives
7 common expressions
8 statements: 'when' and 'how' before 'where'